Your Own Second Home In Europe

Third Edition

Originally written by
Cheryl Taylor

Rewritten and updated by
Steenie Harvey

Your Own Second Home In Europe
Third edition

Published by Agora Ireland Publishing & Services Ltd.

Originally published by Fleet Street Publications Ltd., 103 New Oxford Street, London WC1A 1QQ, UK.
Second edition 1998
First edition 1996

Copyright © 2004 by Agora Ireland Publishing & Services Ltd., 5 Catherine Street, Waterford, Ireland.

Written by: Steenie Harvey
Publisher: Kathleen Peddicord
Managing Editor: Lynn Chestnutt
Copy Editor: Rose Burke
Graphic Designer: Susan Redmond

Cover photography courtesy of Photodisc

Printed by PMR Printing, 45685 Oakbrook Court, Sterling, VA 20166-9298, USA.

ISBN 0-9547754-0-6

Your Own Second Home In Europe

Table of Contents

CHAPTER 3—GREECE

CHAPTER 4—ITALY

CHAPTER 5—MALTA AND GOZO

CHAPTER 6—PORTUGAL

CHAPTER 7—SPAIN

Introduction

Somewhere in Europe the ideal home is waiting for you. That might be a half-timbered cottage deep in the apple-blossom countryside of rural Normandy...an Andalucian village house in one of Spain's traditional *pueblos blancos*...a seaside villa in sunny Portugal...an apartment in elegant Paris or buzzy Barcelona...a bungalow in Cyprus or a House of Character in Malta. For some, it might be a chalet in a twinkly Swiss alpine village or a traditional sugar-cube house with deep blue shutters on a Greek island. And have you ever dreamed of living in Prague... or Budapest...maybe even Warsaw?

An affordable retirement location? A vacation home? A place to invest? A property you can rent over the winter...or for longer?

But first, some points that need careful consideration. Do you want your new property to be a real home (vacation or year-round) for you, or is your aim to generate a regular stream of rental income? If you intend to make your European home pay for itself, then location is of paramount importance. Would you prefer to be by the sea, in a city, or in a quiet location far removed from the madding crowds? Remote rural properties have their charms, but these may not be obvious to most people looking for a place to rent for their vacation.

Do you want a place that is ready to move into, or are you happy to undertake some structural DIY...maybe quite a lot of restoration?

And, of course, how much is your house-buying budget? If necessary, will you be able to obtain a mortgage? Property is a serious purchase, not something to be undertaken lightly. At the end of the day, the price is undoubtedly going to be the most important factor of all.

To help you find your own second home in Europe, we've investigated hundreds of properties in a whole range of countries. We've delved into the Mediterranean sunshine islands of Cyprus and Malta, and also the Greek mainland and islands. We've explored Italy and France, Spain and Portugal. We've also looked at Switzerland...foreigners can now purchase property in some areas of this most beautiful of Alpine countries without having to obtain residency permits.

And we've also investigated Europe's emerging markets. With a whole bunch of former Eastern Bloc countries set to join the EU in 2004, property markets in these countries may be poised to explode. We take a look at the Big Three: the Czech Republic, Hungary, and Poland.

But whatever corner of Europe appeals to you, once you've decided to buy a home, we urge you to engage the services of the following:

- An attorney or other real estate expert to represent your interests to the sellers and their real estate agent.

- A financial expert to counsel you about financing and help you obtain it.

We recommend you contact London-based John Howell & Co, solicitors and international lawyers who specialize in European property transactions. In the past 20 years they have dealt with thousands of transactions in Italy, France, Spain, and Portugal...and now other countries including the Czech Republic and Cyprus. They work closely with U.S. lawyers Marcell Felipe who can advise on tax issues affecting U.S. citizens as well as international real estate.

- **John Howell & Co.**, *The Old Glassworks, 22 Endell St., Covent Garden, London WC2H 9AD; tel. (44)20-7420-0400; e-mail: info@ europelaw.com; website www.europelaw.com.*

In some European countries, non-EU buyers may find it difficult to obtain financing from banks and lending institutions. Where possible, we have given contacts and sources in each particular country, but we cannot promise they will dole out mortgages just for the asking. The director of *International Living's* Paris office tells us that most U.S. buyers who obtain mortgages in France actually obtain them from British lending institutions. Keeping that in mind, it may be worthwhile contacting a UK-based European mortgage specialist such as Conti Financial.

- **Conti Financial Services**, *204 Church Road, Hove, East Sussex BN3 2DJ, United Kingdom; tel. (44)1273-772-811; e-mail: enquiries@contifs.com; website www.mortgagesoverseas.com.*

For help obtaining a mortage in France, contact our *International Living* Paris office property expert Jocelyn Carregie by email at *ParisProperty@InternationalLiving.com*

Twelve Golden Rules for buying a European property

1. Try not to have too many preconceived notions. It's quite likely you will change any original idea about what constitutes a dream home once you're there on the ground.

2. Visit more than one region in your chosen country.

3. Be prepared to put in some legwork. Europe has no such thing as a multiple listings system. Each real estate agent has their own little cache of properties.

4. Don't put down a deposit on the first property you see. In today's boom markets, you sometimes have to move fast, but try to give yourself a cooling off period. And never, ever, allow anybody to rush you into making a snap decision.

5. Research the local property market. Is there an average price per square foot or square meter? What are similar homes changing hands for?

6. Never sign a contract that you do not understand. If it's in a foreign language that you are unfamiliar with, have it translated.

7. Take advice from an independent local lawyer...or a non-local one who specializes in European property...before signing on the dotted line.

8. Before you purchase, ensure that the title is valid and that the

property has no debts. Your lawyer will be able to do this for you.

9. If you are arranging a mortgage for the property, make sure this is stated in the contract. Include an opt-out clause if the loan doesn't go through.

10. Be aware of the additional purchase costs and taxes levied on property transactions in your chosen country.

11. Open a local bank account and set up standing orders to pay bills and taxes. Failure to pay your annual taxes in countries such as Spain, Portugal, and France could lead to legal action and the possible seizure of your property.

12. Finally, never buy a property just because it seems "cheap." A $2 million property may be a good investment because of the market it's in. A $20,000 apartment may be a bad buy.

Chapter 1

The Republic of Cyprus

An island of pine-cloaked mountains, aquamarine coves, and golden beaches, Cyprus is renowned for long, hot summers. Winters are kind, too, but the weather isn't the only reason why you should consider it.

Living costs are low, most people speak English, and foreign residents can benefit from tax breaks. And although Cypriot property prices have risen over the past few years, you can still snap up small apartments for less than $50,000, and two-bedroom homes with fabulous Mediterranean views for under $200,000.

Home to almost 700,000 people, Cyprus is anchored in the eastern Mediterranean Sea. Because of its large ethnic Greek population, some people think it's a Greek island. It's not...the southern half is an independent Republic, the north is under the control of the Turkish Republic of Northern Cyprus.

Southern Cyprus has plenty of modern trappings, but once you've left the cities behind you enter another world. Along with a network of traditional villages, the Troodos Mountains are home to dozens of frescoed Byzantine churches and monasteries.

An oddity of the island's winter climate is that you can ski in the Troodos Mountains in the morning and laze on the beach in the afternoon. These mountains rise almost 6,400 feet, so it's not surprising they see snowfalls. But down on the coast, temperatures are often in the high 60's and low 70's. Even in February, the landscape starts to bloom with scarlet poppies, tiny purple orchids, and vast swathes of yellow, daisy-like flowers.

The Cyprus property map

Cyprus is a favorite hideaway for Britons—and also for Germans, Scandinavians, and increasing numbers of Russians. There's nothing to stop North Americans buying here...this could be the perfect time to take a stake. With EU entry now agreed, most realtors expect further rises in house values. Buyers who got in earlier have already made big gains. In general, properties in southern Cyprus have doubled in value over the last seven years. Last year saw an average hike of 14%.

In some areas, the rise has been even greater. Around Paphos in the southwest (now with its own international airport), prices have risen 50% in two years. But even here, rises are forecast to continue.

Most expatriates-to-be are in the market for villas, small houses, or maisonettes in residential developments along the southern coast. The most popular areas are around the cities of Larnaka and Limassol on the central southern coastline, and also Paphos in the southwest.

Around Larnaka and Limassol, you'll find the least expensive properties. Take note: these cities are functional rather than prettified...and their beaches are no great shakes either. Much of this central southern coastline is now almost completely encased in concrete. The nicer of the two cities is Larnaka. It has an old town, a palm-lined seafront promenade, a marina, and a lagoon...but its surroundings are heavily industrialized.

Paphos was once a sleepy fishing village of around 10,000 people, set among crumbling Roman ruins. The ruins are still there, but it's now more like a small city than a village. Although there are restrictions on building density, residential developments now stretch into the hills and out beyond Coral Bay. The population has burgeoned to 35,000 and another 25,000 live in the surrounding area. That said, it's the most attractive of the island's resort towns.

But the southern coastline isn't all built up. Midway between Paphos and Limassol, pretty Pissouri is a traditional coastal village of leafy squares and coffeehouses. Here, two-bedroom, low-rise apartments with sea views are selling for $145,000. It's a highly sought-after location, and individual homes don't come too cheap. With unobstructed views of the sea and Pissouri Bay, villas of around 1,375 square feet with private pools are fetching $350,000.

Also consider the northwest, especially around the small towns of Polis and Latchi near the Akamas Peninsula. Relatively undeveloped, it has the best coastal scenery in Cyprus. Much of the area is a national park...keeping large developers at bay.

The southeastern corner of Cyprus has great beaches, but we recommend avoiding Ayia Napa. A full-blown resort town, Ayia Napa concentrates on the cheap end of the holiday package-tour market. From May to October, it's a pulsating partyland for the under 30s. Flashing neon and noisy clubs are one thing, but the excessive drinking and the drugs are another... Having a British army base nearby doesn't help matters either. That said...it's fairly cheap. Resale studios in complexes with pools near the beach start at $39,000, one-bedroom apartments at $46,000, and two-bedroom apartments at $70,000.

Protaras and Paralimni are more family-oriented and the beaches are just as good. This is where you'll find the nicest buys in seaside villas and apartments. Through Cyprus Sun Properties, new two-bedroom apartments on Paralimni's outskirts sell for $79,000.

Village houses cluster the foothills of the Troodos, but bargains are becoming harder to find. Fixer-uppers start at around $50,000 for a small cottage...you'll probably pay at least double that to make it habitable. A fully restored two-bedroom village house generally costs at least $138,000. Restored gems tend to be pricey, especially if they're within easy striking distance of one of the cities. However, traditional homes are usually subject to negotiation, so haggling may bring the price down.

Theomaria Estates has a good selection of village properties. It lists an old two-storey stone-built house, a 10-minute drive from Limassol Beach, at $60,600. With open mountain views, it presently consists of two large rooms and a yard. Converting it into a two-bedroom house is estimated at another $60,000.

Theomaria also lists an old two-storey coffee shop consisting of four big rooms and balcony. Attached to it is a stone-built village house with seven rooms and a small yard. Cost for both properties as they stand is $101,000.

If you're in the market for something "traditional," note that most Cypriot villages don't much resemble the picture-postcard hamlets of Italy, Spain, and France...or the whitewashed, blue-shuttered villages of the Greek islands. Unfortunately, lots of the island's old stone homes were demolished decades ago.

Plenty of Cypriot agents and developers market village houses, but their idea of a "village house" is usually a home in a purpose-built settlement. Some (like in the village of Kamares near Paphos) are very attractive, though others are look-alike and bland.

Few expatriate retirees consider living in the island's divided capital, Nicosia. An inland city, the southern (Greek Cypriot) part of this divided metropolis is mostly anonymous concrete high-rises. The summer heat is far fiercer in the city than near coastal areas...you're more than one and a half hours away from the sea.

But if Nicosia does appeal, prices are still very reasonable for a European capital. Through ForSale.com.cy, a two-bedroom, 1,100-square-foot apartment with views of Nicosia and Pentadaktilos mountain range is $106,000. On the seventh floor of an apartment block with communal pool, it's on the top of Acropolis Hill, right opposite the American International School and very close to all amenities. Restaurants, shops, fast-food chains, and everything you might need are all within walking distance.

Paphos

On Cyprus' southwest coast, Paphos is Aphrodite country and a treasure store of antiquities. The town divides into two separate districts. The part along the coast is known as Kato Paphos—this is the tourist strip. A mile and a half up a hill is Ano Paphos, where most local people live. There's a colorful market in Ano Paphos and a lot more "real" shops.

Overlooked by the western Troodos Mountains, lower Paphos is set around a harbor with an ancient fortress and plenty of fish tavernas. It's prime territory for tourists, most of whom seem to be of retirement age. If you've got any feeling for history, don't miss the Tombs of the Kings, the mosaics in the House of Dionysus, and the huge archaeological park west of the harbor.

Town planners have learned from the mistakes of Limassol and Larnaka...the development program supposedly guarantees that the area's character will be preserved. The cardinal rule: No high rises! Residential developments are generally of higher quality than in the other two towns.

As a result, Paphos is very popular with north European buyers, and prices are higher. But the market is wide. There are literally hundreds of developments with resale, newly built, and off-plan properties...so take your time. Prices obviously depend on the quality of the development, size of property, and the view. This chart, based on listing in the areas, will give you a rough idea of what you can expect to pay in Paphos.

Resale market

- Projects without a swimming pool: $40,000 to $70,000 for one-bedroom apartments, and $60,000 to $110,000 for two-bedroom apartments.

- Projects with swimming pools: $80,000 to $130,000 for one-bedroom apartments, $121,000 to $170,000 for two-bedroom units, and $140,000 to $200,000 for three-bedroom apartments.

- Two-bedroom maisonettes or townhouses: $110,000 to $160,000.

- Three-bedroom maisonettes or townhouses: $170,000 to $242,000.

- Villas vary widely from around $170,000 to upwards of $222,000 for two- and three-bedroom homes.

New developments with use of pool

- One-bedroom apartments: $100,000 to $140,000.

- Two-bedroom apartments: $130,000 to $200,000.

- Three-bedroom apartments: $180,000 to $240,000.

- Two- and three-bedroom maisonettes and villas: $150,000 to $300,000.

- Depending on plot size, custom-designed villas with private pools go from $180,000 for two-bedroom homes to over $1 million for a palatial property. (Most three-bedroom detached villas in Paphos go for $225,000 to $260,000.)

The Garden of Cyprus

The countryside surrounding Paphos is known as "The Garden of Cyprus." Small holdings produce an abundance of grapes, citrus fruits, vegetables, and bananas.

Twenty miles west of Paphos, Pegeia is a purpose-built village with spectacular views of the Mediterranean. Here a two-bedroom resale terraced house (approximately 900 square feet) is listing for $189,000. Air-conditioned throughout, it has rear patio and garden, dining and lounge area, fully equipped kitchen, two twin bedrooms (both with balcony), separate W/C and shower rooms. With views of Coral Bay, the communal pool is just a few steps outside the door. Coral Bay, regarded by locals as the best beach in Paphos, is just a seven-minute drive away. There you'll find most beach activities and more shops, bars, restaurants, and tavernas.

The village of Trimithousa is only a few minutes' drive from Paphos. At the southern edge of the village, the small Trimithousa Panthea development has views down to the coast and lots of green areas. Two miles away at the village of Tala, golfers tee off at Tsada within 15 minutes of leaving the house. Here, two-bedroom semi-detached townhouses (988 square feet) are selling for $180,000.

If you enjoy golf, look at Secret Valley. Twelve miles east of Paphos, this 18-hole course plays to a par 72. The residential village has sea and mountain views, and exclusively designed villas and bungalows are on large plots of 13,000 to 21,500 square feet. Through Aristo Developers, prices for Secret Valley villas start at $333,000.

Also near Paphos, Aphrodite Hills is even swisher. Described as "the first integrated golf, leisure, and real-estate development in Cyprus," it's built on 578 acres of hillside. This really is the top end of the market...it will cost you about $800,000 to buy a 16,000-square-foot plot and villa with around 1,600 square feet of living space and the same amount again in covered verandahs and private pool. A couple of years ago, you could have bought the property for half the price. Even three-bedroom resale villas are now fetching over $500,000.

You may not be smitten with developments in touristy Kato Paphos, but there are some gorgeous villas in the hills beyond town. Designed and built by Leptos, Kamares village was voted one of the world's five best developments by the International Real Estate Federation. Bespoke villas, all with red pantiled roofs have "oh, wow" views over the Mediterranean...and high price tags. A four-bedroom resale villa with two reception rooms and private pool is currently on sale for $891,000.

Polis and the Akamas Peninsula

During summer, loggerhead turtles lay eggs on Lara Beach, a beautiful sandy stretch of the wild and mountainous Akamas Peninsula. Forty miles northwest of Paphos, the Akamas is Cypriot equivalent of a national park.

There are no busy resorts, just miles of undeveloped coastline and hiking trails with some of the island's best views. The sea hereabouts is a limpid shade of turquoise and so crystal clear that you can see the fish swimming about.

Approaching from the Polis gateway, you can take a car only as far as the Baths of Aphrodite, a cave-like grotto with a dark pool where the goddess is said to have frolicked with her young lovers. To get the best from the Akamas, be sure to bring boots or sturdy shoes …paths are too stony for sandals. One of the best walks is along the path at the edge of a cliff…in early spring it's dotted with lilac-colored wild cyclamens.

The closest town to the Akamas Peninsula is Polis, 12 miles distant. Town is a bit of a misnomer. In reality, it's a large village with a shady square full of *kafenions* (coffee shops) and old men sitting clicking worry beads. The tavernas on Municipality Square offer great views of the barber's shop where the brave submit to cut-throat shaves.

Some smaller developers are active around here. A three-minute drive from Polis or Latchi, Prodromi village is a new complex of one- and two-bedroom apartments and two- to three-bedroom maisonettes. Owners share a large swimming pool surrounded by landscaped gardens. The development will also comprise some three-bedroom luxury villas with their own private pools and garden areas. Delivery will be November 2004. (Most new projects in Cyprus sell off-plan.) Apartment prices start at $133,000 with maintenance fees of approximately $50 a month.

A couple of miles from Latchi Beach (beyond lies the Baths of Aphrodite and the Akamas Peninsula) is Lemon Grove…another new development due for completion in late 2004. Through Cyprus Property Network, prices for one-bedroom apartments start at $104,600 and two-bedroom units from $137,700. A central communal swimming pool is planned. All apartments have independent access—the upper ones via an external staircase.

Overlooking Latchi's harbor, and with a private path to the beach, Aristo Developers are building seven exclusive villas. Exclusive prices too…they start at $512,000.

Limassol

Some of the least expensive Cypriot property is on the central southern coastline, around the resorts of Limassol and Larnaka. You can still unearth one-bedroom resale apartments in these cities for around $57,000 and two-bedroom units from $78,000. However, much of the surrounding areas are very built up. Although both Limassol and

Larnaka are popular with Russian buyers, they may not represent your notion of life on a Mediterranean island. Not unless you're seeking bright city lights.

The island's main port and a thriving business center, Limassol is the second largest city in Cyprus. You'll find modern shops and restaurants, a high standard of medical services, and good schools. Although it now seems a jungle of concrete high rises, things weren't always so—it served as a port for two historic city kingdoms: Amathounta and Curium. Both have yielded some rich archaeological finds.

Limassol bills itself as the island's entertainment capital of Cyprus. With its museums, castles, theaters, and galleries...a mammoth spring Carnival and a September wine festival...there's no shortage of culture.

A new complex with communal pool in Limassol called Potamos Germasoyias is 500 yards from the beach. Priced between $63,600 and $131,300, apartments range from 430 to 1,010 square feet.

Peace and quiet is only 25 minutes drive away. In the foothills of the Troodos Mountains, there's a new project in Trimiklini village. Two-storey houses (1,031 square feet) with an additional 139 square feet of verandahs are listing for $188,500 through *ForSale.com.cy*. The project has its own clubhouse with swimming pool and tennis court...the ski center of Troodos is only a 20-minute drive away.

Larnaka

In the 17th century, Larnaka was Cyprus' diplomatic and trading capital. Another remarkably ancient settlement, it rose from the ruins of the city-kingdom of Kition. According to legend, Kition was founded by Khittim, the son of Noah.

Nowadays Larnaka is a modern seaside city, and it will probably be your first stop...this is the location of the island's main international airport. Along with plenty of shops and restaurants, it has several museums, a large harbor, and a yacht marina with 200 berths. Many of its hotels on the golden sands to the east are luxury level, but the views of the city are drably industrial. That said, Larnaka's palm-fringed seafront in the center of the city is attractive.

In Larnaka's McKenzie neighborhood, (a short walking distance to McKenzie Beach, the city center, the Phinikoudes seafront, restaurants, supermarkets, and parks), studios and apartments are available in a new five-storey building. The units range in size from 320 to 1,235 square feet. Prices go from $48,500 to $242,500 for penthouses. It could be a good investment property...there's a high demand for new rental apartments in Larnaka.

Prices fall the further you get from the seafront. In a residential area close to the hospital, three miles from the beach, 860-square-foot apartments are on sale for $97,000, and 1,180-square-foot apartments for $175,700. That equates to $115 to $150 per square foot compared with $155 to $195 per square foot in the McKenzie neighborhood.

Protaras, Paralimni, and Ayia Napa

In the Protaras district of eastern Cyprus, you'll find a development of new two-bedroom individual villas...1,040 square feet, sea views, on a plot of 2,340 square feet...for $200,000. This villa development is close to unspoiled countryside, traditional windmills, contrasting coastlines...and only 200 yards from a beautiful sandy beach at Ayia Trias.

Part of Paralimni municipality, Protaras has experienced huge growth and development during the past 15 years. However, stricter government controls have ensured that its ecological charm and character haven't suffered too much. Some of the most beautiful beaches on the island are in this area, the most popular being Fig Tree Bay.

Through Cyprus Property Network, the Ayia Triada Beach Gardens project is right on the Ayia Trada seafront, a short stroll from a beautiful sandy beach and picturesque harbor. Less than one mile east of Paralimni village, it lies between the seafront and the coast road connecting Paralimni and Protaras. Larnaka Airport is only 35 minutes drive away on a modern two-lane highway.

Building has not yet started, but already 25% of the development has been sold from plan. If this beach location were on the Paphos/Polis side of the island, homes would probably be at least 50% more. Prices for three-bedroom villas (1,353 square feet) on a 2,150-square-foot plot start at $222,000.

Also in this area, Karoullas and Markoulis Estates have a string of projects that include villas of all types and sizes, single and two-storey terraced houses and maisonettes. Prices range from $86,800 to $606,000.

Finally, if you are a party animal, by all means head to Ayia Napa and check it out. Current bargains through Cyprus Sun Properties include a two-bedroom detached resale villa with small garden in a residential area for $136,000.

Cypriot realtor and developer contacts

- **Leptos Estates,** *111 Ap. Pavlos Ave., Paphos; tel. (357)26-880-100; e-mail: info@leptosestates.com; website: www.leptos.com.cy.*

- **Aristo Developers,** *8 Aprilou 1st St., Paphos; tel. (357)26-811-600; e-mail: market@aristodevelopers.com; website: www.aristo developers.com.*

- **Cybarco** (Head Office), *Dhali Zone, P.O. Box 21653, 1511 Nicosia; tel. (357)22-741-300; e-mail: info@cy.cybarco.com; website: www.cybarco.com.*

- **ForSale.com.cy,** *1 Lord Byron Street, Office 101, 1046 Nicosia; tel. (357)99-584-999; e-mail: sales@forsale.com.cy; website: www.forsale.com.cy.*

- **Karoullas and Markoulis,** *Protaras-Paralimni, P.O. Box 133, Cyprus; e-mail: pmarkoulis@cytanet.com.cy.*

- **Theomaria Estates,** *P.O. Box 54282, CY3722 Limassol, Cyprus; tel. (357)25-372-917; e-mail: sales@theomaria.com; website: www. theomaria.com.*

- Other useful websites for Cyprus property are *www.easyrealestate cyprus.com, www.cypruspropertynetwork.co.uk,* and *www.cyprus sunproperties.com.*

Rentals

If you're seeking a long-term let, you can rent studios and one-bedroom furnished apartments in most areas for under $3,000 annually. For a three-bedroom villa, the starting figure is around $12,000 a year. Most agents handle rentals as well as sales.

For $445 monthly, Theomaria Estates currently has a two-storey fully furnished detached villa with a small, private walled yard in the Paphos-Kouklia area. Nine miles from Paphos, the villa is only 200 yards away from the sanctuary of Aphrodite and has unobstructed mountain and sea views. Secluded beaches are only two miles away and you're also near Secret Valley Golf Course.

Another very reasonable rental is available through *www.cyprus-property.net*. This two-bedroom house is in Panagia, a mountain village resort only a half-hour drive from Paphos and the coast. Recently renovated, it has a modern equipped kitchen, big sitting room, an extra room (presently used for more formal occasions), and a bathroom. The house is fully furnished, including TV, video, and air conditioning. It also has a large stone-paved yard and garden, veranda, and garage. There are few properties near the house…the noisiest neighbor is the donkey living in back of the house. Including free donkey wake-up calls, monthly rent is $505. Other listings on the website include:

- Fully furnished studio apartment in a house in the mountain village of Panagia, $404 monthly.

- Two-bedroom fully furnished apartment in Larnaka, two minutes from the center of the town. Open-plan kitchen includes washing machine, cooker, and fridge, $606 monthly.

- New three-bedroom house in the quiet Strovolos neighborhood of Nicosia. Central heating, veranda, small garden front and back, sheltered parking at $707 a month.

- Three-bedroom, two-bathroom house in Ayia Napa, within walking distance of Nissi Beach, $1,212 monthly.

- Three-bedroom luxury villa in Limassol, $1,414 monthly.

What potential buyers should know

Cyprus' status as a former British colony means that almost all the population speaks English as well as Greek. Of course, like in many outposts of empire, the downside for North Americans is that everybody drives on the left-hand side of the road...

The island has lots going for it, but it won't suit everybody. Summers can be debilitating and some retirees find the heat unbearable...as well as the hordes of biting insects. "You couldn't live without air-conditioning," says one man who always returns to the UK during July and August. In these months, daytime temperatures can reach 110° F. It's also very humid.

Water shortages have occurred during recent summers. Tourists in the posh hotels didn't suffer, but most residents got their water switched off at least twice a week. The good news is that new desalination plants are now in operation, and the water problem has supposedly been solved.

Regarding developers, a huge number of small, one-man bands have set up shop. There are some cowboys about. If you're thinking of a new-build property, we advise you deal with members of the Cyprus Real Estate Agents Association, or those affiliated to FIABCI, the International Real Estate Federation.

The political situation also needs mentioning. If you don't follow world events, it's easy to get the impression that Cyprus is entirely composed of ethnic Greeks. It's not—the island is divided by what's known as "the Green Line," a buffer zone manned by U.N. peacekeeping forces.

In 1974, the northern third of the island was occupied by Turkish forces, and now goes by the name of the Turkish Republic of Northern Cyprus. While the Republic of Cyprus is a safe-enough haven for visitors and prospective residents, bitterness still remains between the two sides.

Restrictions

Despite EU entry, property laws haven't yet been liberalized in the Republic of Cyprus. You still cannot buy more than one property. Non-Cypriots are only entitled to freehold ownership of either an apartment, a house or villa, or a plot of land up to three donums in size (about 43,000 square feet). A moratorium restricting EU buyers from freely buying property has been granted for five years.

Technically, non-EU buyers must seek permission to purchase property from the Council of Ministers after signing a contract of sale...but this permission is granted as a matter of course to all bonafide purchasers. Your agent or lawyer can apply on your behalf.

Buying your home

Like the country's legal system, the Land Registry department follows the British way of doing things and so title deeds are secure. Larger realtors have their own in-house legal departments. If you hire your own lawyer, they charge from $800 to $2,000 in fees, depending on the work involved.

A once-only property transfer fee is payable to the Land Registry. The first CYP 50,000 ($101,000) of property is levied at 3%, the next CYP 50,000 at 5%, and anything above that at 8%. Sounds complicated...but on a purchase price of CYP 140,000 ($282,800), property transfer fees would be CYP 7,200 ($14,540).

Government stamp duty is due within 30 days of signing a contract. Purchasers are charged 1.5 CYP ($3.03) per thousand up to the value of CYP 100,000 ($202,000). Thereafter the rate is 2 CYP per thousand. In general, you should allow an additional 7% of purchase price to cover taxes and fees.

Obtaining finance

You are required to pay in foreign currency, but the entire cost doesn't necessarily have to be paid at the time of purchase. Easy payment terms and in-house finance schemes are available from the larger developers. With Leptos, for example, the usual terms are 10% down, another tranche of 15% three months later, with the remaining balance paid in 12 to 36 monthly installments. After delivery of the villa, only a maximum of 9% interest is applied on a reducing-balance basis.

Commercial banks in Cyprus are authorized to offer mortgage facilities to assist the purchase of property. For foreign buyers, the loan is in foreign currency: euros, dollars, and pounds sterling. The amount lent ranges from 60% to 80% of the value of the property with a repayment period ranging up to 20 years.

Residency permits

North American citizens don't need visas for up to 90 days. If you intend taking up residence, you'll need a residency permit. People who have bought property tell us they've encountered no problems in obtaining one. The granting of the permit is based on an ability to support oneself.

To obtain permanent residency, you must apply to the Committee of Aliens Control. You have to agree not to work, and you must show an annual income of at least CYP 3,800 ($7,676).

You can also apply for permanent residency under the category of a self-employed foreigner...if you want to open your own business in Cyprus. The condition is that your operations will not hurt the local economy. The minimum capital required is CYP 150,000 ($303,000).

- **Embassy of the Republic of Cyprus,** *2211 R Street NW, Washington D.C.; tel. (202)462-5772 or (202)462-0873.*

Cost of ownership

Annual property taxes levied by the government depend on the property's value. Most residents don't pay anything. Property tax is calculated on market values from the year 1980. On properties up to CYP 100,000 ($202,000), there is no tax. On properties valued at CYP 100,000 to 250,000 in 1980, tax is 2%.

This anomaly means that even on a resale property that sells today for CYP 200,000 ($404,000), there is no property tax. Chances are that it was probably valued at less than CYP 100,000 in 1980. If a house was built after 1980, market values of the year of purchase are adjusted downwards to take account of the inflationary index.

You will pay some tax, however, to municipal authorities. They levy an annual property tax of about $40 to $80 per year. Some authorities also impose a sewage tax of $40 to $80, again depending on the value of the property.

If you buy into a development, you'll have to pay common charges. Usually payable monthly or quarterly in advance, they vary from development to development, and depend on the area and type of property. Charges cover a share of the cost of cleaning and maintaining common areas and gardens, swimming-pool upkeep, electricity in common areas, management fees, rubbish collection, and repairs. The annual total is usually $500 to $900.

Cost of living

Living costs in Cyprus are low...around two-thirds the cost of similar European good-weather destinations. Once you've bought a home, bills are minimal. Many expatriate couples enjoy a comfortable lifestyle and a fairly active social life on an annual income of around $16,000... $20,000 and the living is even easier.

Annual costs in Cyprus

- Home maintenance and annual taxes: $1,100
- Utilities: $660
- Groceries: $5,200
- Meals for two twice per week in a modest taverna: $1,800
- Car tax and insurance: $570

Groceries will cost a couple around $100 a week. Water and electricity costs depend on usage, but the average for most couples is $400 per year for electricity and $260 for water.

Regarding telephone installation, tenants have to pay a refundable deposit of around $210 for a landline. Property owners pay no deposit. The connection fee is $45...a three-minute call to U.S. is around $1...a local call is $0.04 per minute. Standard dial-up Internet is $14 monthly through Cytanet.

Insuring your home will cost in the region of CYP 2 per thousand of the sum insured. For example, on a $200,000 home, insurance is around $400.

Medical care in Cyprus is very inexpensive. A doctor's visit costs about $20 to $40...X-rays from $28...a prescription is $12. Yet, the quality of health care is very high...the majority of doctors are trained in the UK and the United States. Private medical insurance costs around $50 monthly. All residents of Cyprus, whether Cypriot or not, can take out local private medical insurance.

Dining out is around $9 to $11 per person for cheap and cheerful...$27 for gourmet. A cinema ticket costs $7.40...one-mile taxi ride is around $2.

Paying your taxes

Cyprus has treaties for the avoidance of double taxation with a number of countries including the United States, Canada, and the United Kingdom. This ensures that tax isn't paid twice in both countries.

Until recently Cyprus taxed expatriates a flat rate of 5% on remittances. Many foreign residents kept their assets growing free of tax in an offshore bank or trust, and simply brought in what they needed.

However, to comply with EU requirements, tax laws have been changed. The government now taxes worldwide income for residents ...and domestic income for non-residents. Individuals are considered to be residents of Cyprus if they stay for more than 183 days on the island during a particular calendar year.

For all Cypriot tax residents, total annual income up to CYP 10,000 is tax-exempt. Beyond that, income of CYP 10,001 to 15,000 is levied at 20%...CYP 15,001 to 20,000 at 25%...and income of CYP 20,001 and up at 30%.

When you want to sell

If you want to sell your property at some time in the future, all of the proceeds can be repatriated, including the value of the purchase price, any amounts spent on capital improvements, as well as profits and any interest earned. Capital gains are taxed at 20% on gains in excess of CYP 10,000 ($20,200). The inheritance tax was abolished in 2000.

Chapter 2

France

An island of pine-cloaked mountains, aquamarine coves, and gold All the glories of Paris—and a lot more besides. France is a country of snow-capped Alpine peaks, stylish beach resorts, and a glorious green and golden interior where ancient towns cast shimmering reflections into lazy rivers.

So many locations rightly belong in an art gallery. Brittany...a land of stone-built cottages, blue hydrangeas, and wild seascapes... Alsace...storybook wine villages, half-timbered cottages straight out of Hansel and Gretel... Sun-kissed Provence...old honey-tinted farm-houses...a magical landscape of sunflowers, lavender fields and silvery olive groves.

Jewel after jewel. The medieval walled towns of the Dordogne and the Languedoc...the quaint harbor towns and apple orchards of Normandy...the castle-studded Loire Valley...the vineyards of Bordeaux...the bewitching island of Corsica, Napoleon's birthplace. Think how much easier it would be to get to know these regions if you owned your own home here...

But it's not simply splendid landscapes. There are feast days, fairs, and festivals. Then there's the culture, legends, and long centuries of history. It's the feeling you get when you're exploring a medieval town...that you've somehow fallen through a crack in time and re-emerged in the High Middle Ages.

And it's all those civilized pleasures the French have got down to a fine art. The wonderful food and long dinners that linger for three hours...the entertaining conversations...the stylish films that dare not deign to insult a cinema-goer's intelligence...

What's more, prices in many regions are amazingly low. In northern and central France, numerous properties to renovate can be found for $15,000 to $30,000...or less. Just $11,900 (cement mixer included) is the asking price for a small but structurally sound barn deep in the Limousin region, a tranquil land of hills, meadows, and river gorges. Forest walks, fishing, mushroom hunting, and horse-riding all at your doorstep.

And $28,500 buys a two-bedroom house in the heart of a small village (population 150). That's an hour's drive from Brittany's ferry port of St. Malo. Although it has electricity, you would need to install sanitation. But don't let that put you off. We're including it to illustrate just how low prices can be.

Not everybody wants builders tramping over the place. A home you could move straight into? Here's one in central Brittany—a two-storey house with two bedrooms that used to operate as the village forge. Only a short stroll to the boulangerie and other local shops, it's $67,500.

For $95,600, you could buy a comparatively modern house in an old hamlet, deep in the Poitou Charentes region. Good structural condition, two bedrooms, large garden—all the house needs is some interior decoration. The hamlet is just a few minutes' drive from the village of Bussiere Poitevine, which has regular farmers markets and street markets...even a livestock market twice a month.

Thought Provence was beyond your budget? Although the Riviera is certainly not for the financially challenged, villages in mountainous Haute Provence still turn up bargains. Here's a ready-to-move-into cottage, ideal for an outdoorsy couple into skiing, hiking, horseback riding, and water sports. The nearest ski resort, open from Christmas until early spring, is 20 minutes away. The area has a range of man-made lakes for water activities. With views of the mountains from its terrace, the one-bedroom cottage has a large fireplace (all you need to heat the whole property) and a brand-new fitted kitchen with beautiful tiles. Price: $62,500.

A pad in Paris?

Romance...history...culture...shopping. The City of Light has everything you could possibly want from a European city: theaters, opera and art-house cinemas, world-class museums and galleries, flea markets and sophisticated shopping, imposing architecture and grand palaces, and chic cafés. Even neighborhood restaurants serving five-star fabulous food and wine.

The very names of its *arrondissements* (neighborhoods) resonate with centuries of history. Saint Germain and the Latin Quarter... Montmartre and Sacre Coeur...the Opèra, Notre Dame and the Île de la Cité ...the Champs Elysées, the Marais, and Bastille...

The best property buys aren't necessarily the lowest-priced. Paris has 20 arrondissements and square-foot prices within each vary enormously. Some neighborhoods have tremendous cachet...others aren't quite so desirable.

As throughout the rest of France, prices are always in square meters, not square feet. However, to make things easier, we've done the math for you. At the time of writing, the average square-foot price in Paris as a whole stands at around $420. With prices starting at around $290 per square foot, the 10th, 11th, and 19th arrondissements are the most affordable parts. But at the more rarefied end of the price scale, you can be paying $1,600 per square-foot for a top-quality apartment in a prime arrondissement.

The Île Saint-Louis, right in the heart of Paris and the site of Notre Dame, is the number one most requested spot for those seeking short-term rental apartments. Marble plaques on the facades indicate several illustrious former inhabitants such as Madame Curie, Charles Baudelaire, and sculptor Camille Claudel. The area around Pont Saint-Louis and Pont Louis-Philippe is incredibly romantic...and in the lit-up evening, one of the most stunning spots in all of Paris. On the Pont Saint-Louis, which is closed to traffic, musicians and street performers are a regular attraction.

Property here is very expensive, and often quite difficult to find. Apartments often reach $1,120 per square foot. A two-room, 615-square-foot apartment on quai d'Orléans—with a fireplace, *parquet de Versailles,* and a view of the Seine—is currently being advertised for

$660,000...a bit of a bargain to some buyers. As good properties sell in less than three weeks, you must be prepared to move fast.

One thing that usually surprises North Americans is how small Parisian properties are. But remember that space is relative...even in the U.S. A one-bedroom apartment in Texas is likely to be larger than a one-bedroom apartment in New York City...and all European cities have different notions about apartment size.

A Parisian studio can be as small as 55 square feet or as large as 430 square feet. A one-bedroom...called a *deux pièces* or two rooms (for the bedroom and the living area)...is usually from 375 to 645 square feet. A two-bedroom or *trois pièces* is usually 535 to 970 square feet. Three-bedroom apartments and larger range from 860 square feet to 2,150 square feet...and so on.

If space is what you want, you'll need a big budget, but you'll get a break. Per square-foot, larger apartments are usually less expensive than their smaller counterparts.

If you want location, then be prepared to pay for it. However, you can expect solid appreciation that outlasts the tests of time. And Paris has lots of time. Its buildings dating back to the 16th century are solid...and they aren't being razed to make room for some new sprawling complex.

But what will you get for your dollars? Is it possible to buy anything for under $100,000?

Certainement! We found three that were once *chambres de bonnes* (servants' quarters). Small, admittedly, but they can be great first footholds into Paris...a spot to call your own while you're here...or to rent to students.

- Studio in the 10th arrondissement: one-room apartment of 105 square feet on rue de Paradis in a fine 17th-century building. Entry code system and concierge. This studette is on the 5th floor with an elevator. Access by principal staircase. In the mansard of the building with velux windows for extra light, shower, wardrobe, cupboard, and kitchenette. Repainting required. Price: $42,000.

• Studio in the 9th arrondissement: South-facing studio with a floor surface of 215 square feet or 120 square feet according to the Loi Carrez (a strict law governing the measurement of a property's livable space. An apartment measured according to *Loi Carrez* does not include stairways, terraces, balconies, etc., or any floor space with a ceiling lower than 1.8 meters). Near Saint-George Métro station.Two louvered windows. With shower, WC, wash basin, sink in kitchen area. Rental report shows 8.75% return. Price: $48,000.

• Studio in the 16th arrondissement: Between the Trocadéro and Place Victor Hugo, with a view of the Eiffel Tower. Former service room, 65 square feet, with wood paneling and a water point. On the seventh floor with an elevator. Double-glazed windows. $37,200.

Rentals for students are in short supply. No matter how meager the living space...even if it's the size of a broom cupboard...an apartment in almost any arrondissement will attract students since on-campus accommodation is practically non-existent. Gross yields are currently 5% to 8%. A property costing $100,000 and leased at $500 per month represents a gross annual yield of 6%...not even taking into account capital appreciation of around 10% per year.

Of course, a student broom cupboard is unlikely to prove the ideal home for even the most minimalist-minded buyer pining to relocate...or for vacationers seeking a short-term rental. Some, however, might be tempted by the Bohemian romance of Montmartre. Being billed as a "buy-to-let" investment, Conseil Patrimoine has studios and one-bedroom apartments in a classic newly refurbished building that is a five minutes' walk from place du Tertre and with views over to Sacre Coeur. Studios of 215 square feet start at $144,000.

For foreign buyers—and visitors—the most appealing apartments are in older residences built in the typical Haussmannian style. Those are the decorative stone buildings featuring large windows with iron-work balconies and parquet flooring.

But location is paramount for a Paris apartment to have good short-term rental value. This means it needs to be located near the center of the city. The most desirable areas for renters...and thus buyers... are the 1st, 3rd, 4th, 5th, 6th, 7th, and 8th arrondissements. These are also some of the most expensive areas to buy into. Average cost for the 6th and 7th arrondissements is $660 per square feet, $555 per square feet for the 5th, and $535 in the 4th. Remember, though—they're only averages.

Described as "the perfect foothold," a fully refurbished large studio in a building in the Marais (3th arrondissement) dating back to the 17th century. With beamed wooden ceilings and 375 square feet of living space, it's close to all kinds of bars, shops, and restaurants. Price: $252,600.

Right at the center of the Latin Quarter, near rue Mouffetard (renowned for its foodie market) and rue des Ecoles, a 505-square-foot, one-bedroom apartment in a classic Parisian stone building in mint condition. The living room, with exposed wooden beams, faces the street; the bedroom looks out on the inner courtyard. Price: $326,400.

Within walking distance of the Champs Elysées, in the 8th, a typically Parisian two-bedroom apartment (580 square feet) is $528,000.

In the heart of literary Saint Germain, ideal for rentals, a 666-square-foot, one-bedroom apartment in a recently cleaned and restored stone building. $636,000.

- For details of current Paris listings (those here are on offer as we go to press), contact *International Living's* Paris property expert by e-mail: *ParisProperty@InternationalLiving.com.*

Brittany: Celtic France

Some of France's best-value properties are in the northwest, in the province of Brittany. Though the beaches are fantastic, one of the reasons why prices are so much lower than in the south of France is the cooler weather. *Bretagne* is very much northern Europe. Expect it to be fairly rainy in the winter.

Imbued with legends, Brittany is France's Celtic fringe. From the megalithic standing stones at Carnac to Merlin's mysterious Forêt de Brocéliande with its associated Arthurian legends, this truly is a land shrouded in mystery.

It's also beautiful. Open to the sea on three sides, the region's 800 miles of jagged cliff-top coastline are a lovely succession of little walled towns, oyster beds, and fishing ports. If you enjoy folklore, wild places, and aren't too concerned about year-round sunshine, you'll fall head over heels in love with it.

While low-priced renovation properties abound, it doesn't cost a fortune to purchase a home you can move straight into. The following gems are all currently on the market with Guegan Immobilier:

- Near Callac in central Brittany, a ready-to-live-in, two-storey house with stone-fronted façade. Four bedrooms and bathroom on the upper floor, a kitchen, two large rooms, and a utility room on the ground floor. There's potential to do up the attic, too. Price: $42,500.

- A lovely village house, a 45-minutes drive from the Golf du Morbihan. On the ground floor is a main room with kitchen corner, a living room with exposed wooden beams, and fireplace that opens onto a small garden. Upstairs, a mezzanine and bath room. An outbuilding is included in the price of $57,600.

- In central Brittany near the lake of Guerledan, bordering on the Quénécan Forest, is a house that was the village bar and super-market. It could still be used like that, or as a house. There is a new roof, a bar, kitchen, another large room, boiler room, cellar. On the upper floor are two rooms, three bedrooms, a bathroom, toilets and an attic above. All windows are new, and there's a small courtyard at the back. Price: $70,400.

- Close to Lamballe, and just 15 minutes from northern Brittany's beaches, a semi-detached stone cottage on a 1/4-acre of land, ready to live in. Kitchen with fireplace, a bedroom, another room, bathroom, toilets, and utility room—with the possibility to do up the attic. Has garage and outbuilding. Price: $80,500.

- On the outskirts of Ploermel, one hour from the St. Malo ferry harbor, a little house decorated with attractive red-and-white brickwork around its windows. Ready to live in, it has a garage and garden of 6,500 square feet. Basement with cellar and utility room; ground floor with two large rooms, bathroom, and toilets; first floor with three bedrooms. Price: $110,600.

- Up the price to $141,000 and you can have a traditional Breton stone longère—a long, low, stone-built farmhouse. Near Près de la Chapelle, 15 minutes from the lake of Guerledan in central Brittany, this *longère* has been nicely renovated. It has a fitted kitchen, bathroom, living/dining room, and a downstairs bedroom. Upstairs are three more bedrooms and a bathroom. Land amounts to 3/4 of an acre.

- $161,000 buys another beautifully renovated *longère* in southern Brittany, a 10-minute drive from Josselin. With garage and outbuildings, this farmhouse has a kitchen, living room with fireplace, bathroom, toilets, and utility room. On the first floor are two bedrooms, plus room enough to create three more and another bathroom. If you want a *longère* to renovate, traditional Breton farmhouses in reasonable structural condition start at around $50,000.

- **Guegan Immobilier,** *2 rue St Gilles, 22000 Brieuc; tel. (332)96-33-29 -30; e-mail: property@wanadoo.fr; website: www.brittany-property.com.*

Norman conquests

Clouds of apple blossoms...groves of beech trees glimmering sapphire with bluebells...foals gamboling in meadows...plus...an array of delectable homes at affordable prices. Fringed by 400 miles of coastline, Normandy is Brittany's next-door neighbor—and it's just as appealing.

Apple orchard and cider country, *Normandie* sports great sandy beaches and the English Channel...which the French call *La Manche.* Resorts include Deauville and Trouville, and there are some quaint, old-fashioned harbor towns such as Dieppe, and Honfleur with its cobbled streets and tall, skinny houses.

History comes at you in a deluge. Caen was William the Conqueror's birthplace and little more than an arrow-flight away is Bayeux, site of the famous tapestry depicting the Norman Conquest of England. With a pretty *vieille ville* (old quarter) of timbered houses, Rouen was where Joan of Arc burned at the stake.

Among Normandy's patchwork of meadows and trout streams are gorgeous cottages, farmhouses, and manor homes clad in overcoats of half-timbering. Laid over stucco walls, the black or brown wooden strips are often shaped into intricate patterns. The French call this distinctive architectural style *colombage*. Quite a few half-timbered homes have thatched roofs too. Fabrice Blacher currently has an *ensemble normand* on its books: three *colombage* cottages that have been renovated into one principal home and two gîtes (vacation accommodations). On around an acre of land, this package is $179,000.

You can pay less...or more...for a *colombage*-fronted home along the coast. For $72,000, Guy Hoquet agency has a sweet little cottage—refurbished and with a stripy timber front—just 200 yards from the sea at Villers sur Mer. Wonderful, if you can manage with just 325 square feet of living space. For $92,400 is a tiny *maison de bourg* (town house), with brown-and-white timbered front, and inside, two principal rooms plus kitchen and bathroom. The maison, in a village between Trouville and Honfleur although only a couple of minutes from the beach...but there's no sea view.

If you need that all important sea lookout, a six-room cottage has a listing price of $423,000. Seems mad when you could buy an authentic 16th-century manor house for less...ones in good condition start at around $393,000 in this area.

Overall, prices are a little higher along the Normandy coast than in Brittany. For one thing it's much closer to Paris, and the resorts of Deauville and Trouville are very popular for French weekend getaways. A one-bedroom apartment with a five-minute walk from Trouville's beach is $99,000. At Deauville you can easily pay $117,000 for 355 square feet of living space. Any kind of property near the coast is generally priced to reflect the area's desirability. Most renovated two-bedroom cottages will be around the $100,000 mark, sometimes more.

The best Normandy bargains are inland, in the Pays d'Auge countryside radiating out from the pilgrimage town of Lisieux. Small cottages to renovate go from $25,000 to $45,000. For $36,000, you can buy a 750-square-foot *pressoir* to restore on 43,000 square feet of land. A *pressoir* is a farm building where apples get pressed into cider. Some are huge, and they can make comfortable and unusual homes.

Ready-to-move-into cottages and houses in the Lisieux area are amazingly good value...especially since most still have romantic *colombage* facades. Current buys on the market include a 375-square-foot cottage for $80,400 and an 840-square-foot townhouse for $82,800. For $117,000, you could buy an absolutely charming *colombage* and brick two-bedroom cottage (750 square feet) with a small flower-filled garden. And should you fancy apartment living, one-bedroom apartments (344 square feet) in Lisieux town can be found for $40,800.

- **Agence Fabrice Blacher,** *1 rue de la République, 14600 Honfleur; tel.(33)2-31-14-00-00;e-mail: fabrice.blacher.immobilier@wanadoo.fr.* (Other agencies are at *91 rue Eugène Colas, 14800 Deauville* and *8 Place F. Moureaux, 14360 Trouville.*)

- **Guy Hoquet,** *61 rue Henri Cheron, 14100 Lisieux; tel. (33)2-31-48-28-48; e-mail: lisieux@guyhoquet.com; website www.guy-hoquet.com.* To access Lisieux properties on the website, type in the code 14100 on the home page.

Provence—the Alpes Maritime

Quaint hilltop villages and a sunshine coast. The Riviera playgrounds with their palm-lined promenades...quieter seaside towns where locals gather in shady squares to play *pétanque* (an outdoor type of bowling). The Camargue marshes where black bulls roam wild alongside white horses. Wonderful cities like Marseille, Nice, Arles, Aix-en-Provence, and Avignon...Provence has the lot.

But first let's look at the French Riviera, the famous Côte d'Azur. Admittedly any villa with a sea view will sell for a fabulous price. Most of you would probably be buyers at the lower end of this villa-with-a-view market. Your dream home would have between 1,950 and 2,150 square feet of living space...its own grounds...a pool. You'll find a choice of properties like this for $900,000 to $1.1 million...but you can pay one heck of a lot more than that for a villa.

Happily not all properties are so ostentatiously priced. The apartment market is effectively a nest of micro-markets with varying prices from resort to resort...and often a range of prices within each resort itself. Certainly an average-square-foot price for various types of property along the Riviera exists. It starts at $233 for studios—typically with living space of 280 square feet. For one-bedroom apartments averaging 420 square feet, it's $218. For two-bedroom apartments averaging 655 square feet, it's $215. For three bedrooms (1,030 square feet) and larger units it's $275.

Based on those averages, you can calculate ballpark figures of $65,000 for studios, $91,500 for one-bedroom units, $141,500 for two-bedroom properties, and $285,000 for a three-bedroom apartments. However, as you can imagine, "averages" don't give the full story.

A Nice lifestyle

Nothing is average about Nice, for example. (If you can't imagine living without city lights, this could be your ideal home away from home.) Like most big cities, it comes wrapped in an overall package of expensive neighborhoods, up-and-coming areas, and parts that are downright insalubrious.

Anywhere near the Promenade des Anglais with a Mediterranean lookout will be expensive. However, prices are more sensible once you get into the heart of *Vieux Nice:* the old town with its *rue piètonnées* (pedestrianized streets), Cours Saleya flower market and Place Garibaldi, the Musiciens quarter—all are respectably bourgeois as is the old port with its renovated and new-build residences.

Neighborhoods in the hills—like Mont Boron—have wonderful views over the city to the sea and Cap Ferrat, but they tend to be pricey locales. You'll certainly pay dearly for traditional authenticity and charm. On the top floor of an old Mont Boron mansion, a three-bedroom sea-facing apartment (1,290 square feet) with an additional 752 square feet of terraces goes for $914,000.

At the other end of the scale, some of Nice's cheapest properties can be found in the outer suburbs: a 430-square-foot apartment in the Liberation quarter is $66,000. Streets around the railway station are also cheap. However, unless you fancy setting up home in a neighborhood where sleazy-looking hotels rent rooms by the hour, the station neighborhood is unlikely to appeal.

Overall, the square-foot average for Nice's property market is slightly lower than the regional average. But, as always, it all depends on location. And you can't get a better location than the Palais de la Méditerranée, an up-market development with an Art Deco façade on the Nice seafront. Here apartment residences are priced from $425 to $630 per square foot. The smallest one-bedroom overlooking the Promenade des Anglais will set you back at least $178,000. Bigger one-bedrooms go for a lot more.

On the other hand, many one-bedroom apartments in new developments to the east and west of Nice are selling from $110,000 to $130,000. Through Beaumont Immobilier, prices for a one-bedroom apartment "in perfect state" start at $126,000. A couple of steps from Place Garibaldi, in the heart of old Nice, a one-bedroom is $138,000. For an absolutely immense *deux pièces* of 880 square feet with a little garden, in the Musiciens quarter of central Nice, the asking price is $269,000.

If you're seeking a long-term rental, one-bedroom properties in Nice and its environs go for between $490 and $575 monthly.

More Côte d'Azur resorts

From Hyères to the Italian border, 26 resorts line the Côte d'Azur. Some resorts are now more mass transit than jet-set, and a good deal of the coast is under concrete, but others retain a class ambience. The villas on Cap Ferrat are as palatial as ever, the Antibes marina is packed with yachts, and the glitterati still flock to Cannes every May for its film festival.

But the Riviera's image is changing. Outside the summer season, one of every two trips here is business-related. Convention centers and trade fairs abound, and the region is also noted for being a high-tech hive. The Sofia Antipolis science and technology park near Antibes is home to over 1,200 French and foreign companies involved in micro-electronics, telecommunications, computer hardware and software, mobile telephony, e-business, health care, and Internet-related technologies.

Again, prices in the different resorts are across the board. A view of the sea and the palm-lined promenade from the terrace of a 625-square-foot, one-bedroom apartment in Antibes? You can have it for $401,000. Directly in front of the plage de la Salis beach in the heart of Antibes, here's another one: a 535-square-foot apartment in a guarded residence for $312,000. On the other hand, $116,500 is the asking price for another one-bedroom unit with an easterly exposure. It is located at the beginning of Cap d'Antibes rather than in the town.

If you are in the market for a Riviera villa, Azur Riviera has one with pool and 11,000 square feet of grounds, built in the typical Provençal farmhouse style of pink stonework and wooden shutters. A few minutes from Antibes town center, with 2,365 square feet of living space, it has two lounges, five bedrooms and garage. Price: $1.01 million.

Between Monaco and the Italian border, Menton of the flowery villas and lemon trees is one of the Riviera's prettiest resorts. You could rent a 560-square-foot apartment here for $625 a month. To buy? Well, a 485-square-foot apartment in town is listed at $168,000 and a 775-square-foot apartment at $233,000. But over towards Roquebrun Cap Martin, prices are even steeper. A studio with 420 square feet of living space is $210,000. Goodness knows how much of that price goes for the view…over the bay and across to the Principality of Monaco.

In the hills behind Menton in Gorbio, a 15-minute drive from the sea, Elit'Immobilier has a 430-square-foot apartment with beamed ceilings and corner fireplace in a traditional village house. Built on a rocky crag, Gorbio is a typical village perché (literally a perched village). Priced at $120,000, the apartment looks west to the mountains.

- **Beaumont Immobilier,** 7 *rue Beaumont, 06300 Nice; tel.* (33)4-93-56-66-46; *e-mail:* contact@beaumontimmo.com; *website: www. beaumontimmo.com.*

- **Acetimo,** 1 *avenue Mirabeau, 06000 Nice; tel.* (33)4-93-62-62-08; *e-mail:* contact@acetimo.com.

- **Azur Riviera International,** 26 *boulevard Maréchal Leclerc, 06600 Antibes; tel.* (33)4-92-93-60-60; *e-mail:* contact@azur-riviera-international.com; *website: www.azur-riviera-international.com.*

- **Elit Immobilier,** 33 *avenue de Verdun, 06500 Menton; tel.* (33)4-93-28-57-28; *e-mail:* contact@elitimmobilier.com; *website: www. elitimmobilier.com.*

Rural Provence

The Riviera's hinterland holds out a wonderful contrast to the busy coastal resorts. Stitched together by country lanes and silvery olive groves, rural Provence is the dreamscape land of Van Gogh and Cezanne...neat pink farmhouses with wavy-tiled roofs...summer lavender...and sunflowers. Medieval villages perch on craggy outcrops like something from a Perrault fairytale. Many villages are even older than the castles that crown them, dating back over a thousand years.

Provence is famous for its lavender fields, but meadows are like a wayward cottage garden. Delicate blossoms flower their tiny hearts out: blue and mauve irises, grape hyacinths, pink valerian, dwarf narcissi, scarlet poppies. Pale lilac-colored wisteria wraps up many village houses like gift boxes. And the air... Perfumed with wild herbs, it feels balmy even in springtime.

Adorned with ramparts, narrow streets, flowery balconies and breathtaking views of the Mediterranean, villages near the coast include Eze, Haut de Cagnes, St. Paul de Vence, Mougins, Biot, Tourettes, and Grasse.

Don't expect anything much resembling a bargain if your favorite village is within easy striking distance of the coast. Even modestly sized houses in these villages fetch astounding sums. In the heart of medieval

Haut de Cagnes, with sea views from the upper levels, a bougainvillea-strung house with 1,500 square feet of living space is $456,000.

Through Emile Garcin, one of the most gorgeous properties on the market at the time of writing is a huge *mas* (country house) at St. Paul de Vence. Built in 1590, it's in very good condition, has around 4,300 square feet of floor space with kitchen/living space opening onto a terrace, two living rooms, a dining room, laundry, six bedrooms, four bathrooms, and an independent studio. Provençal charm includes quarry tiles, fireplaces, an old dovecote...and...in the enclosed grounds of almost an acre...a large swimming-pool. Asking price is a fraction over $2 million.

For houses under $100,000, you'll have to venture far from the beaten Provençal track. The British agency VEF (*www.vefuk.com*), which has local agents on the ground, has some great buys in Haute Provence. For example, $62,500 buys a two-bedroom house in Serres, a riverside village with butchers, bakers, a pharmacy, bars and restaurants, water park, and supermarket. Built on the side of a south-facing hill, it's surrounded by mountains and fruit orchards. The two-storey house has a new roof...all it needs is a fresh coat of paint.

- **Agence Emile Garcin,** *avenue Jean-Charles Mallet, 06250 Mougins; tel. (33)4-97-97-32-10; e-mail: cotedazur@emilegarcin.fr; website: www.emilegarcin.com.*

Corsica—France's scented isle

Exactly 106 sea miles from Nice, the sun-kissed French island of Corsica is the Mediterranean—as it used to be. A land of honey bees, lemon groves and vineyards...small seaside towns unspoiled by development...mountain villages that have survived the centuries intact...no mass tourism.

Carpeted in aromatic herbs, it's one of Europe's most beautiful islands. In fact, it's probably the most beautiful of them all: The sea shimmers with jade and blue hues. Red and pink coastal outcrops have been weathered into an architectural fantasy of arches, columns, and pinnacles. Beaches glitter gold and silver. In pastel-washed coastal towns, garden walls spill over with clouds of bougainvillea, wisteria and other bright Mediterranean flowers.

Beyond the coastal shade of palm trees and umbrella pines, Corsica's interior is equally dramatic. Shaped by the elements into spires and needles, dizzying granite mountains soar above thick chestnut forests. Waterfalls cascade in silver spangles down steep rock faces and icy torrents race through deep gorges.

Untamed though the landscape looks, this is also a land of *villages perchés*: stone villages straight from medieval woodcuts. Dozens of tiny stone settlements perch on crags or cling precariously to steep hillsides. Some even seem to have wedged themselves inside cracks in the mountains.

Split into two *départements* (provinces) called Haute-Corse and Corse du Sud, Corsica has 40% of its 260,000 inhabitants living in just three areas. In the southwest, seaside Ajaccio is the capital and home to around 60,000. In the northeast, Bastia boasts a population of 38,000 and is the second city. Next comes Porto Vecchio in the far south—but with less than 11,000 inhabitants it's hardly a megalopolis. Everywhere else is the size of a village.

On the island's northwest is a region known as the Balagne. Tagged "the Garden of Corsica," the rolling pastures between the sapphire sea and the mountain foothills form the island's main farming area. Here Calvi, home to just 5,000 inhabitants, huddles beneath its citadel like the perfect russet-roofed Mediterranean toy town. Over three miles of sandy beach spread out under shady pine trees beyond its harbor and sailing school. Cobbled back streets conjure up restaurants offering everything from stuffed squid to hearty boar-meat stews. And the season is punctuated by jazz festivals…fireworks extravaganzas…and plenty of *manifestations nautiques* (boating fairs and competitions.)

Through Calvi's Agence Medimmo, small studios (of around 270 square feet) start at $63,600. One that's being sold fully furnished has 450 square feet and a price of $100,500. Villas go from $350,000 to just over $1.2 million.

East along the coast, the port town of Île Rousse is also a center for beach life and water sports. It gets its name from the tiny rust-colored islets offshore. The main gathering point is Place Paoli, a huge square bordered with 100-year-old plane trees where people at pavement cafés watch local grandpas playing *boules* (lawn bowling). New-build apartments here are similar to those in Calvi, costing around $235 per square foot.

There are some inexpensive homes in Balagne mountain villages, but villa-type properties rarely surface for under $300,000. At Monticello, a village three miles in the hills above Île Rousse, a 1,100-square-foot villa lists for $346,000.

If you're seeking a holiday home for yourself...or to rent...a bijou apartment for $77,000 at Lumio may fit the bill. Wonderful sea views...but living space only amounts to 365 square feet. Lumio is the village east of Calvi. A larger 860-square-foot apartment, also with a sight of the sea from its terrace, is $220,000.

Six miles from the coast, in Aregno village, $51,200 is the asking price of a stone-built *maison village*. It's in good condition but you don't get much *maison* for your money. Living space is only 460 square feet. Medieval folks really did tend to build on the doll's house scale. While there are mountain views from a back room, you'd have to crouch to see them through the tiny window.

An Aregno studio apartment is $49,400. From its terrace, there's a grandstand panorama of the sea beyond the olive groves and orchards spooling below. However, at 175 square feet, it's even more cramped than the *maison village*. Even so, it might make a holiday home for minimalists. During July and August, tiny studios easily achieve weekly rents of $360. Something more spacious? At Speloncalato, a 1,600-square-foot *maison village* with five bedrooms and two bathrooms is $173,00. Encircled by mountains, this is cave country: the village takes its name from the Corsican word for grottoes, *spelunche*.

In south Corsica, Bonifaccio is a spectacular fortress town, perched atop dazzling white cliffs never breached by invaders. Nowadays, frequent ferries make the hour-long crossing between Bonifacio and the

Sardinian town of Santa Teresa di Gallura.

Between Bonifacio and Porto Vecchio, Nice agency Conseil Patrimoine is offering a new development with guaranteed rental income. Their management company forecasts gross yields of 11% on eight months' letting per year. (For studios, indicative weekly rents start at $365 in March and April rising to $640 in July and August.) Near a beach and marina, the fully furnished properties will range from studios to three-bedroom duplexes:

- Studio of 335 square feet plus 130-square-foot terrace, from $106,600.

- One-bedroom of 545 square feet plus 225-square-foot terrace, from $144,500.

- Two-bedroom of 750 square feet plus 215-square-foot terrace from $192,000.

- Three-bedroom duplex of 965 square feet plus 300-square-foot terrace from $258,000.

Realtor contacts

- **Agence Medimmo,** *Centre Commercial Madonna di a Sarra, 20260 Calvi; tel./fax (33)4-95-60-72-19; e-mail: info@medimmo.net; website: www.medimmo.net.*

- **Agila Immobilier,** *Avenue J. Calizi, 20220 L' Île Rousse; tel. (33) 495-60-55-48; website: www.agila-immobilier.com.*

- **Conseil Patrimoine,** *52, boulevard Victor Hugo, 06000 Nice; tel. (33)4-97-03-03-33; fax (33)4-97-03-03-34; website: www.french-real-estate.com.*

Guaranteed returns from the French Leaseback Program

In terms of tourist numbers, France is one of the world's top destinations. Popular destinations such as the Riviera, Paris, and ski resorts in the French Alps have a shortage of quality tourist accommodation. The French government has consequently come up with a number of plans to encourage investments in tourist rentals. One of these is leaseback.

Through the leaseback program, you can purchase qualifying property free of valued-added tax—19.6% in France. This means a $100,000 property is immediately discounted to $83,600. And you can arrange financing for up to 95% of the purchase price at a fixed interest rate of 6%. Money can be available for up to 20 years.

Although you own the property outright, you agree to turn it over to a property management group for rental for a fixed number of years (typically nine). In return, you are guaranteed a net return on the rental of between 4.5% and 6% after all management and operating expenses have been deducted. Plus, you've got capital appreciation. Properties qualifying under the Leaseback Program are in the country's most popular areas and so are the most likely to appreciate.

In some cases, during the nine years that the management company is letting your property, you get use of it for two to four weeks a year. This, though, depends on the property and the management company. Some allow you two weeks use annually, some four, some don't allow owner use at all—so this is an important point to clarify upfront. However, guaranteed returns generally go down the more weeks you're allowed.

Leaseback has nothing to do with timeshare. Only approved companies can offer plans. Those that do are usually subsidiaries of leading French companies. You buy a freehold apartment and are the legal owner. It's registered in your name in the land registry and at the end of the lease-back period, the property is yours...to do with as you please. You can continue to rent it out, use it yourself, sell it or possibly start a new lease.

By using leverage, you invest a relatively small amount and yet reap the gains on a large amount. Assuming the bank lends 80%, your own money can be geared fivefold, multiplying the potential return by up to five times. Rental incomes come in monthly...convenient for repaying the loan. If you don't want to move to France just yet, this could be an interesting way of getting a toehold in the property market.

Properties under the leaseback program run from $50,000 for a studio in the Pyrenees to more than $1 million for a villa on the French Riviera. Opportunities at the time of writing include a development in the Alps at Saint Gervais, a traditional ski village under the shadow of mighty Mont Blanc. At the development, a studio apartment of 290 square feet is $102,300; a one-bedroom apartment of 425 square feet, $157,000; a two-bedroom apartment of 520 square feet goes for $189,000; and a three-bedroom apartment duplex of 745 square feet is $270,000.

In a residence overlooking Monte Carlo, Conseil Patrimoine is offering studios and apartments with a guaranteed rental income of 5% net over the nine-year term. All apartments have panoramic sea views. Studios are from $196,800; one- and two-bedroom apartments start at $300,000.

In Cannes, one of the most sought-after destinations on the Cote d'Azur, Imoinvest has leaseback properties—all with balcony—in a luxury residence with large swimming pool. It's 100 meters from the beach. Prices start at $84,000 and go up to $312,000 for two-bedroom apartments. Net rental income is 4.5%.

The chateaux-filled Loire Valley is less than two hours from Paris. Near the city of Tours, Imoinvest also has another luxury residence on a historical site with pool, spa, etc. Prices for one- and two-room apartments are from $96,000 up to $146,400 with net rental income of 4.5%.

• **International Living** Office in Paris: *ParisProperty@International Living.com*.

Rentals

Paris can be tricky for budget-minded foreigners seeking a long-term rental, particularly furnished properties. While it's fairly easy to find short- to medium-term furnished rentals, you will likely pay $2,000 to $4,000 per month for even a one-bedroom property in the most prestigious areas—the ones everybody wants to rent in. (Which goes to show what can be achieved if you buy an apartment. Choice one-bedroom properties often rent at $1,200 or more for the week.)

For $3,200 monthly, Cooper Paris Flats has a one-bedroom apartment with queen-sized bed and sleeper sofa (sleeping two to four) in the heart of the historic Marais district, just behind Place de Vosges. A few feet away from the Arc de Triomphe, the Champs Elysées, and the Poncelet open-air market, another one-bedroom apartment is $3,700.

Locaflat has this one for $2,375 monthly: "Excellent location in the Latin Quarter next to the river Seine, in an 18th-century building. The apartment is on the third floor, no elevator, 25 square meters (300 square feet), one bedroom with double bed, living room with sofa bed, kitchenette, washing machine, bathroom, and WC. Recently refurbished with wood beams and antique flooring. Telephone, cable TV. Métro: Mabillon, Odeon, Pont Neuf (lines 10 and 4)."

But if you're prepared to compromise on location, reasonable deals exist. This next rental is through Casaland, which also has links to Paris agents on its website.

"In rue Damrémont (Paris 18th arrondissement—Métro lines 12 and 4), nice apartment to rent as from the first of February. In its surface of 375 square feet, you'll find an equipped kitchen (fridge, hotplates, and cupboards), a living room, and a large independent bedroom with two wardrobes. Windows with double glazing, view on the courtyard. Charges: 656 euros ($787 monthly) all included."

Of course, locals don't use expat agencies. They'll be calling into specialized French rental agencies or checking classifieds in *Le Figaro*. Or, just the same as with buying property, they'll go to a French *immobilier,* a real estate agent—many also handle rentals. However, most *immobiliers* in Paris only handle apartments in their immediate neighborhood.

The norm is to sign a one-year lease for furnished properties and a three-year lease for unfurnished properties. Rent is usually paid monthly in advance, but the owner cannot demand more than two months' rent as a deposit. Providing no damage is incurred, this deposit must be returned to the tenant within two months of the termination of the lease.

Long-term rentals along the Côte d'Azur are 30% to 40% below what they are in Paris. Monthly rents for studios in Nice are mostly between $420 and $530; in Cannes $490 to $640; and in Antibes $550 to $650. One-bedroom apartments in Nice run from $530 to $600; in Cannes from $620 to $825; in Antibes from $730 to $915. Two-bedroom apartments in Nice from $825 to $1,190; in Cannes from $825 to $1,370; in Antibes from $1,000 to $1,370. A house or villa is from $1,100 to $3,300 on up.

In Rouen, Normandy (where Joan of Arc was burned at the stake), studio apartments range from $200 to $355 monthly. In Villers sur Mer in Normandy, monthly rent for a one-bedroom apartment with sea view from its balcony is $395.

- **Porter Scott,** *ParisRentals@InternationalLiving.com.*

- **Locaflat,** *63 Avenue de la Motte-Picquet, 75015 Paris; tel. (33)1-43-06-78-79; website: www.locaflat.com.*

- **Casaland,** *website: www.casaland.com.* A good countrywide website for finding links to agents with rentals (and sales, too).

How to find a realtor

More than 8,000 French agents belong to FNAIM (*Fédération Nationale de l'Immobilier*). FNAIM can provide you with a list of member agents in your chosen area. The organization's website has a comprehensive listing of agents and a database detailing properties available in any given area: *www.fnaim.fr.*

With so many British buying in France, there is a whole niche industry of property agencies. Britain-based VEF (*Vivre en France*) has agencies all over France with agents on the ground from Brittany to Aquitaine to Provence. Some of the listings are wacky, but they always seem to give an honest description.

- **VEF (UK) Ltd.**, *4 Raleigh House, Admirals Way, London E14 9SN, Britain; tel. (44)20-75-15-86-60; e-mail: info@vefuk.com; website: www.vefuk.com.*

Our Local Office in Paris is there to help you...

It's easy to find a bunch of French real estate agencies in any town ...the hard part is finding ones who can speak good English. Whether you're looking to buy or rent, *International Living's* Paris office can help you with any aspect of setting up home in France. If you want to deal with people who know North Americans, and have experience in what they are looking for, get in touch with: *France@InternationalLiving.com.*

What potential buyers should know

Be sure that you understand France's inheritance laws before signing any legal documents. How you structure any contract (whether it is in a single name, joint names, or the name of a company) affects who inherits your property. Regardless of how you've formulated your North American will, don't assume that your spouse—or anybody else—will be the beneficiary of your French property when you die. France's complex inheritance laws date back to Napoleonic times and guarantee children (and sometimes parents) a share of the estate. A spouse has no automatic right of inheritance. There are ways around this—a specialized lawyer can advise you.

Although it's quite rare, some French houses or apartments have what's called a *viager* attached to the title. You may have heard of Jeanne Calment, a native of Arles. She made world headlines a few years back for a couple of reasons...

The first was her incredible longevity. When she died in 1997, she had reached the age of 122. But when she was 90, she had negotiated to sell her apartment *"en viager."* It means "for life" and this is how the deal worked: Monsieur Raffray, the man who bought Mme. Calment's apartment, planned to move into it after her death. He also agreed to pay her 2,500 francs per month for as long as she lived. (At the exchange rate of the time, around $500.) He naturally assumed that he wouldn't be paying the viager for too long.

But Mme. Calment lived on...and on. In fact, Monsieur Raffray died at the age of 77, without ever occupying the apartment. In total, he had paid out what then equated to $184,000 in handouts to the old lady for a property he never got to live in. And his survivors were legally bound by the agreement. They still had to write Mme. Calment her monthly check. "In life, one sometimes makes bad deals," mused the cigarette-smoking, foie-gras-eating Mme. Calment.

Buying your home

The buyer is responsible for all legal costs and government fees or charges for property transfers. These vary, depending on whether you buy a new home or an older property. Generally, though, you can expect to pay 9% to 10% on resales, and 3% to 4% for a newly built house or apartment.

Sales tax may be payable for properties under five years old where there has been no previous sale. This tax is normally included in the quoted price of a property. But as it's 19.6%, you should obviously make very certain that you are not liable for it.

It is difficult to give an exact total for purchase costs, as the agency fee (usually 5% to 8%) can be paid by either party—in some cases it's split. And sometimes homes are advertised with the agent's fees already built into the selling price.

Sample purchase costs for a $100,000 resale property
Purchase tax (4.89%)—$4,890
Notarial fees (3% to 4%)—$3,500
Geometrist's costs—$240
Lawyer—$1,700
Estate agency fee (8%)—$8,000
Total—$18,330

If agency fees are already accounted for—and you decide against using a lawyer—total purchase fees will come down to around 9%.

Before signing the title deed (*acte de vente*) with a French *Notaire* (notary) it is usual to sign a preliminary binding contract (*compromis de vente*) which commits both seller and purchaser to the deal…or a *promesse de vente* which is an option to purchase by the buyer. This contract, subject to the parties' terms, is usually prepared by a real estate agent.

A 10% deposit is usually required when signing the first contract. On completion, the balance of the purchase price is payable—usually through the notaire's account—along with the notaire's fees and stamp duty. Stamp duty varies according to the type of property. It is generally about 6.5%, payable on completion. The conveyancing process usually takes a minimum of two months to carry out local searches.

Obtaining finance

Unless you're already a resident in France…and you have a salary or some other income going into a French bank account regularly…you are unlikely to get a loan from a traditional French bank. As a foreigner, your best bet is with British lender Abbey National…or the former British lending institution the Woolwich—now taken over by Banque Patrimoine & Immobilier (BPI). Both have experience working with foreigners who need a mortgage to purchase property in France. If you are a resident, you may be able to finance up to 80% of the purchase price; if you're a non-resident, up to 70%.

According to Abbey National, the monthly payments for all loans and rent (including your Abbey National France loan) should not exceed 30% to 33% of your joint or single pre-tax monthly income. See the bank's website at *www.abbey-national.fr.*

Residency permits

If you're a U.S. citizen wishing to live in France for more than three months, **before you move** to France you need to obtain a visa from the closest French consulate in your home country or current country of residence. It isn't possible to arrive as a tourist and then change status to that of a resident. The authorities will require you to return home to apply for the appropriate visa. Once you arrive in France, you'll also need to register with the police and obtain a residency card or *carte de séjour.*

- **Consulat Général de France,** *4101 Reservoir Road NW, Washington, D.C. 20007-2185; tel. (202)944-6195.*

Cost of ownership

Annual property taxes consist of the *taxe d'habitation* (paid by owners-occupiers and most long-term rental tenants) and the *taxe foncier* (real estate tax). For a studio or one-bedroom apartment in most cities, *taxe d'habitation* is around $240. The calculation formula is quite complex and varies depending on whether the property is your primary or secondary residence. Secondary residences are taxed at a higher rate.

The *taxe foncier* is based on the value of the apartment. It takes into account the age of the building, the area of a city, and the size of a property. For example, a Paris studio in an older building in the Marais (3rd arrondissement), with approximately 215 square feet, has been assessed at $205. The *taxe foncier* for a 535-square-foot, one-bedroom apartment in an older building in the 5th arrondissement is $240.

But for a studio apartment and a village house in Corsica, realtors quoted combined annual property taxes of $120 and $360 respectively. Here one- and two-bedroom apartments in coastal towns are likely to be nearer $720 annually. For a small village house in mainland France, your combined bill for the *taxe foncier* and the *taxe d'habitation* will probably be around $500; for a larger house around $1,000.

Apartment buildings in France are similar to co-operative and condo buildings in the States. You own your apartment but share responsibility for common parts of the building with other owners. There is a monthly *copropriété* (co-op) fee that pays for expenses involved in maintaining the building, common utilities (usually including water for all apartments), garbage collection, maintenance, etc. This charge runs approximately $120 per month for both of the above mentioned Parisian apartments.

Charges tend to be lower in provincial cities and towns. In Nice, monthly service charges for most one-bedroom apartments in good residences are mostly between $65 and $90.

Cost of living

Not counting rent or mortgage payments, a single expatriate probably needs around $17,500 to $22,000 a year to run a small home and get the most out of Paris. Less in the provinces. Of course, as always, a lot depends on your own lifestyle. For example, you can get three-course lunches—even in Paris—for $12. Dinner in many small neighborhood restaurants can be had for $20. But if you live in a huge swanky apartment, frequent establishments adorned with Michelin stars, and only drink magnums of *premier cru champagne,* then you'll need rather more than $17,500.

Utilities (gas, electric), though separate state-owned entities, have unified customer operations. In other words, one bill pays it all. In northern France, monthly costs for studios and one-bedroom apartments run $60 to $75 per month, around $120 for larger apartments. It's less in the warmer south. Basic telephone service is approximately $25 per month plus a per-unit fee for each call.

Beyond those basic utilities you may want Internet access and cable television. Prices for Internet access are similar to those in the States. A dial-up service costs around $25 per month but you'll also be paying per-unit fees for telephone usage. Broadband access via cable or ADSL is readily available. After initial modem and set up costs, these services run around $55 per month. The cost for basic cable TV starts at around $25 per month and goes up depending on how many channels you want.

Should you fall ill, you can be assured of first-rate service. According to the World Health Organization, French citizens enjoy the world's best healthcare. If your insurance doesn't cover doctor's fees, visits will be in the region of $30.

Although private health insurance is mandatory for North American expatriates, you may be able to transfer your plan to a French provider. Some British companies also provide cover for individual expatriates. Costs depend on age and medical history, but if you're in good health, monthly premiums average $180.

You could also join the Association of Americans Resident Overseas and buy into their group plan. For residents, the annual premium for the most comprehensive plan for 30- to 49-year-olds is about $2,450.

- **The Association of Americans Resident Overseas,** *34 avenue de New York, 75116 Paris; tel. (33)1-47-20-24-15; fax (33)1-47-20-24-16; e-mail: aaromail@aaro-intl.org; website: www.aaro-intl.org.*

Paying your taxes

If you spend less than 183 days a year in France then you are classed as a non-resident. However, you must pay income tax on any earnings derived from activities in France. That includes any income from letting property, wherever it is received. For non-residents, it will be a minimum of 25%.

Foreign nationals are considered residents for tax purposes if their home, principal place of abode, professional activity, or economic interest is located in France...or if they live in France for more than 183 days per year. Resident individuals are taxed on worldwide income, subject to applicable tax-treaty relief. French income tax is levied from 7.05% to a maximum 49.58%:

French income tax rates
On income of 4,191 to 8,242 euro ($5,029 to $9,890) the rate is 7.05%.
From 8,242 to 14,506 euro ($9,890 to $17,407), 19.74%.
From 14,506 to 23,489 euro ($17,407 to $28,187), 29.14%.
From 23,489 to 38,218 euro ($28,187 to $45,861), 38.54%.
From 38,218 to 47,131 euro ($45,861 to $56,557), 43.94%.
Above 47,131 euro ($56,557), the rate is 49.58%.

An annual wealth tax (*impôt de solidarité sur la fortune*) is levied on individuals with worldwide wealth exceeding 720,000 euro ($864,000). For non-residents, wealth is assessed only on French assets. The rate is progressive, from 0.55% to 1.8%, on assets above 15 million euro. Business assets are exempted.

When you decide to sell

If your French property is your permanent home...and provided you spend at least eight months there each year...and you live there for more than five years...you are not subject to the capital gains tax. As with many tax issues, it's a complicated subject so we recommend you seek specialist advice. For most second-home owners, the tax is levied at around 33% after accounting for inflation relief and improvement costs.

French inheritance tax is payable by beneficiaries. The rates and any tax-free thresholds depend on the relationship between the beneficiary and the deceased. For example, children do not pay more than 20% of the value unless their share exceeds 520,000 euros above the tax-free threshold of 46,000 euros. Again though, consult a specialist with knowledge of the French tax system. In France, children have automatic rights of inheritance...but there are ways to get around this.

Chapter 3

Greece

Island Odysseys and the Peloponnese

In toytown harbors, weather-beaten fishermen repair bright yellow nets. Donkeys clop down steep alleyways and wayward goats try to scrabble up into olive trees. White houses cascade with jasmine...cats of every color doze away on terraces...ya-yas (wizened old ladies) sit in doorways shelling peas and exchanging gossip. And the Aegean Sea is as idyllic as in Homer's day: mother of pearl at dawn...deep blue at midday...shot-silk at twilight.

Greece is gorgeous. Of its hundreds of islands and islets, 166 are inhabited—so there is bound to be an island for you. Or consider the Peloponnese mainland—stunningly attractive, but barely known to North Americans. Though the islands are undeniably appealing, overall the mainland offers better value.

That said, you can buy attractive stone-built homes—brand new—for under $80,000 on some islands. Small village houses to restore start at around $25,000...you often find ready-to-move-into village houses for under $60,000.

Compared to other Mediterranean countries, the cost of land in most parts of Greece is low. Athens aside, prices generally range from $12,000 to $30,000 per 1,000 square meters (almost 11,000 square feet). But plots close to the sea are more expensive...a close-up view of the Aegean can cost $72,000 and more.

Building costs vary according to the simplicity or complexity of a planned property...whether it's a plastered or stone-built house ...the size and number of floors...quality of finishing, etc. On Crete, for example, a typical newly-built two-bedroom house of 965 square feet is around $116,000, plus plot costs.

Overall, the average cost for a new house is $110 per square foot…but averages don't tell the full story. On the islands, a useful guide for a fully fitted plastered house of one or two floors is more like $110 to $145 per square foot inclusive of licenses and national insurance for construction workers. (On some parts of the Peloponnese mainland, construction costs fall to around $90 per square foot, but you'll pay a hefty premium on Hydra where everything has to be ferried in.) Construction time is usually six to eight months. Building permits are roughly 4% of the building cost and usually included in the architect's quote.

Stone-faced houses normally cost $145 to $180 per square foot. Count on a construction taking eight to 12 months. More luxurious homes can cost up to $225 per square foot.

If you want to restore an existing stone house or ruin, planning permission is not required if the property is habitable…unless there are going to be significant extensions. For renovation costs, the rule of thumb is to double the property purchase price. If you have paid $30,000, then it will probably cost another $30,000 to renovate.

Crete

More than just a vacation paradise with long, hot summers, myth-laden Crete is as near to Africa as Athens. At 180 miles long, it's Greece's largest island and the fifth largest in the Mediterranean. This is an island of soaring mountains and deep gorges…fertile valleys of orange orchards and olive groves…golden beaches framing clear blue seas. You'll find Byzantine chapels, monasteries, and ancient palaces that seem lost in the Minoan past…but also lively towns and traditional villages where life continues in the same hospitable way as centuries ago. And there's a wide choice of affordable properties.

Chania

In Crete's far west, Chania is the greenest region, overlooked by the

25-mile-long range of the White Mountains. There's some tourist development, but it gets far fewer visitors than the central strip. If you're seeking a peaceful retreat, over 500 villages cling to the mountainsides.

Chania town looks out toward the intensely blue Cretan Sea. Along with a spider's web of back streets and a half-moon harbor, there's a Venetian lighthouse, Turkish minarets and an old waterfront mosque. The cross-shaped market is a wonderful source for Cretan herbs and honey, as well as fresh fish, meat, bread, and cheeses.

West of Chania is a string of small resorts: Platanias is the pick of the bunch. East of Chania is the chunky Apokoronas peninsula...an unspoiled landscape of caves, virgin ravines, shepherds' paths, and traditional villages with views across olive groves to the blue sea. Most Chania real estate agents have plots and houses around here.

Midway between Chania and Kastelli, High Grove is a new development of one-, two-, and three-bedroom houses starting at $75,000. The beach is only three minutes away by car...but you don't have to drive...you can walk through olive groves and bamboo-lined lanes to the sea.

Chania area property sampler

- Restored two-storey Venetian house (800 square feet) in Vouves village where there's a 2,000-year-old olive tree. West of Chania, Vouves gazes across a verdant landscape to the sea and Kamissiana where there's sandy beaches. Price: $106,800

- House of 700 square feet (two bedrooms and two bathrooms) in Old Chania's Upper Halepa neighborhood. Includes small roof terrace and yard. Price: $108,000

- A house with white walls, blue shutters, beamed ceilings, stone floors. There's a restored olive press, and courtyard. It's tucked away from the road through a Turkish archway. Less than a mile from a beach and three miles from Chania, the house has central heating, solar panels, and 1,850 square feet of living space. Price: $150,000

- Renovated under the supervision of Chania's archaeological authorities, "the Bishop's Residence," is a 1,500-square-foot house built during the 16th century Turkish occupation of Crete. Formerly a Greek bishop's residence, it has three floors, enclosed courtyard, and is close to the Venetian harbor. Price: $264,600

Contacts for Chania

- **Europa Real Estate** (Johanna Frohlking), *Daskalogianni 68, Chania 73100, Crete; tel. (30)28210-23111; fax (30)28210-23113; e-mail: johanna@europa-crete.com; website: www.europa.crete.com.*

- **Hellenic Homes** (Ioannis Skevakis), *Mitropoleos Square, Chania 73100, Crete; tel./fax: (30)28210-23460; website: www.hellenic homes.com.*

Rethymnon

Midway along Crete's northern coast, Rethymnon is also good for property hunters. With its narrow streets, harbor girdled by fish tavernas, headland *fortezza* (fortress) and lighthouse, Rethymnon Old Town has bags of old-world charm with hole-in-the-wall barbers, workshops, and traditional coffeehouses. Some buildings are Venetian, dating back to the 13th century. You'll also see the pencil-thin spike of a minaret, evidence of when the Turkish Ottoman Empire controlled Crete.

Both a resort and modern working town of 40,000 inhabitants, Rethymon has an eight-mile sandy beach. Beyond lies a spectacular hinterland of mountains, gorges, and ancient sanctuaries. Like elsewhere, there's the option of purchasing traditional houses or building new.

Constructing new villages alongside traditional ones is only just beginning to take off in Crete. The Norwegian realty and construction firm Kreta Eiendom is spearheading the concept around Rethymnon. It also sells village houses, and has architects and builders to design homes to Scandinavian comfort standards. Excluding plot price, single family homes (ready to move into) work out at $110 to $155 per square foot. Luxury villas with private pool are $155 to $225 per square foot.

Pigi is its first full-blown development project. Five miles from Rethymnon, it's a 40-unit development with large communal pool set in olive groves. A quality development styled on an "ideal" Cretan village, each home is solar-paneled and air-conditioned. All are airy and spacious...but none are exactly the same in shape or stonework. Some have gardens...some sun terraces...some have both.

Prices go from $110,000 for an apartment with 635 square feet of living space, an additional 635 square feet of terraces, and a pocket-handkerchief garden. So far, 12 different nationalities—including Greeks—have bought.

As well as arranging legalities and financing of 60% to 70%, Kreta Eiendom offers a letting service. Quality rental properties on Crete are scarce and you could achieve $720 to $840 weekly for a two-bedroom Pigi property during summer. (Winter rates are $480 to $600 monthly.)

Kreta Eiendom's next project is Adele—a development of 35 houses, each with sea view. It aims to create a white village of curved stairways, alleys, and fruit gardens. Beside a river gorge, it's a splendid location. One house has sold off-plan already. Prices for a 1,100-square-foot house with an additional 1,160 square feet of terrace, patio, and garden start at $208,000.

Rethymnon area property sampler

- 6,445-square-foot plot with permission to build a house of 2,150 square feet in Eleftherna village near an ancient archaeological site. On a hill, the plot overlooks the village, hills, and sea. Price: $14,400

- 385-square-foot ruin with small courtyard to restore in a narrow alley in Agios Dimitrios village, five miles from Rethymnon and two miles from the sea. Price: $22,800

- Small traditional house (475 square feet) in Rethymnon old town, below the Venetian Fortezza, and within walking distance to the harbor, shops, cafés, and tavernas. Price: $108,000

- New house (805 square feet) in south Crete, in Selia village, two miles from the sea and Plakias, and 20 miles from Rethymnon. Price: $117,600

- New house (805 square feet) with small private pool and 1,645-square-foot garden in Ksiro Horio village, less than two miles from Rethymnon and the beach. Price: $180,000

Contact for Rethymnon

- **Kreta Eiendom,** *Arkadiou 1, 74100 Rethymnon, Crete; tel. (30) 28310-21434; e-mail: julia@kretaeiendom.no; website: www. kretaeiendom.no.*

Lassithi

Lassithi is Crete's easternmost province. Picture white houses strung with bougainvillea, windmills and a shimmering turquoise sea...ancient Byzantine churches with dolphins frolicking across mosaic floors and glinting gold icons featuring St. George slaying the dragon.

With views of the former "leper colony" island of Spinalonga, the seaside village of Elounda is amazingly beautiful. Although bargain-priced homes in this small resort are hard to locate, you'll find them in villages in the hills behind Aghios Nikolaos, 10 miles up the road. In Kritsa village, for example, renovated traditional houses can still be had for $48,000.

You'll see tiny houses for $24,000, but they need a lot of work to bring them to acceptable standards. As Don Jones of Crete Home Finders says, "Greek village houses don't generally suit North Europeans without having been renovated." It's doubtful they'd suit most North Americans either.

With 2,000 inhabitants, Kritsa is Crete's largest village. Visitors come to buy handicrafts (lace tablecloths, pottery, etc.) as they're slightly cheaper than in Aghios Nikolaos. But you won't find tourists by the bus-load. Kritsa is a real village with traditional coffeehouses...old men clicking worry beads...and fat, lazy cats snuggled on doorsteps.

On the Gulf of Mirabello, Aghios Nikolaos is Crete's fourth largest town with 10,000 inhabitants, a modern hospital, and good transport facilities. Much of the townscape is the usual Balkan block style, but a pretty harbor gives it the feel of a fishing village. Town beaches are small but the water is crystal blue. Behind the harbor is Voulismeni, the town's "bottomless lake." Surrounded by low ochre-red cliffs, it's linked to the sea by a narrow canal spanned by a small bridge.

Further east is the attractive port town of Sitia and Vai beach. With its white sands, turquoise waters and waving palm trees, it looks like it escaped from the Caribbean. The beach at Kato Zakros is pebbly, but nearby is a ruined Minoan palace and the "Valley of the Dead" where the island's ancient inhabitants were buried in rock tombs.

Lassithi property sampler

- Old house for renovation in Kritsa village. Approximately 535 square feet with valley and mountain views. Price: $24,600

- Only needing minor renovation, a small village house (750 square feet) in Kalo Horio (a few miles south of Aghios Nikolaos) with sea views. Will convert into a nice one-bedroom property. Price: $26,400

- Three-roomed house (750 square feet) featuring two stone arches at Latsida. Needing refurbishment, but electricity and water are connected. Price: $48,000

- At Amoudara, near Aghios Nikolaos, a new villa of 860 square feet on a plot of 5,370 square feet—with great views over the Bay of Mirabello. Price: $138,000

- At Pisokefalo near Sitia, a village property renovated to Northern European standards with two en-suite bedrooms, outfitted kitchen, lounge, courtyard, roof terrace. There's also a guesthouse with double en-suite bedroom, kitchen, and dining/living area. Total area: 2,150 square feet. Price: $156,000.

- Overlooking Aghios Nikolaos harbor, a 1,290-square-foot, first-floor apartment. Price: $222,000.

Lassithi contacts

- **Crete Home Finders** (Don Jones), *13 M. Sfakianakis, Ag. Nikolaos 72100, Crete; tel./fax (30)28410-89494; e-mail: cretehf@acn.gr; website: www.crete-home-finders.com.*

- **Crete-Homes** (Hilary Dawson), *1 K. Tavlas Street, Agios Nikolaos 72100, Crete; tel. (30)28410-28804; fax (30)28410-26233; e-mail: office@crete-homes.com; website: www.crete-homes.com.*

The Argo-Saronic Islands

Aegina, Poros, and Hydra...three islands in the Argo-Saronic chain. The greenest of all Greece's archipelagos, this is the nearest group of islands to Athens. Unless you're seeking complete isolation, these islands offer the best of both worlds. Athens is so easy to reach by hydrofoil, residents can still enjoy big city advantages without having to live among the chaotic traffic and pollution. From Piraeus, the Port of Athens, it only takes 40 minutes on a speedy "Flying Dolphin" hydrofoil to Aegina...commuting distance for many residents. Poros is 60 minutes away, and you can reach the car-free island of Hydra in 90 minutes.

Property prices aren't Greece's cheapest, but $74,000 will buy a habitable stone cottage on Aegina Island. Hydra is more expensive. On both Poros and Aegina, though, it's possible to find pretty traditional houses in the island "capitals" for $120,000 or less.

Aegina offers pine-shaded beaches, Byzantine churches, authentic fish tavernas, ancient temples...and nuts. Yes, the crunching sound you'll hear underfoot comes from people stepping on the shells of pistachios. Home to 11,000 residents, Aegina is Greece's biggest producer of these delicious nuts.

Arced around the waterfront, Aegina town is exceptionally pretty ...all fishing smacks and colorful Neoclassical houses. When the modern Greek state was formed, this place reigned as the nation's capital city. The honor was very brief...the town's moment of glory only lasted from 1826 until 1828.

Properties currently for sale on Aegina include a 1,060-square-foot modern house at Agioi village for $88,000. Within Aegina town, the starting rate for similar sized houses in quiet areas is around $95,000, but you can pay a lot more. One of the cheapest properties currently on the market is a 660-square-foot cottage with a 2,150-square-foot garden at Kavourapetra—$42,250.

There are also possibilities for buying land and building a home. However, each island has its own planning regulations...Aegina is no place to get suckered into buying off the proverbial farmer in an olive grove. For one thing, you cannot build on land planted with olive trees. And on some parts of the island, you'll need a 44,000-square-foot plot to build new. Depending on area, tranches of this size sell for around $120,000 if they have that all important sea view.

- **Aegina Estate Consultants,** *Dimokratias 39, T.K. 18010, Segina Town, Aegina Island, Greece; tel. (30)297-24593; e-mail: diako@ hotmail.com.*

- **Aegina Real Estate,** *Odoz P. Irioti, Aegina Town, Aegina Island, Greece; tel. (30)297-28825; e-mail: info@aegina-realestate.com; website: www.aegina-realestate.com.*

Poros

Poros only just qualifies as an island. A mere 400 feet or so of water separates it from the Peloponnese mainland. Hydrofoils and ferries serve the island from Athens, but little water taxis also scoot across the channel from Poros town to Galatea on the mainland.

Poros is also effectively two islands in one: Speria and Kalavria. Tiny Speria is mostly taken up by Poros town. The island's main harbor, it's a lovely jumble of white houses, waterfront tavernas, and quaint back alleyways.

Cut off from Poros town by a canal and a bridge, the Kalavria part of the island has the best beaches. Set among pine trees and a center for water sports, its main seaside resort is Askeli. There's also lots of smaller sandy coves including the enchantingly named Harbor of Love

(*Limanaki tis Agapis*). Here the water is emerald from the reflections of pine trees which come down almost to the water's edge. Although you can walk to Askeli (it's only about two-and-a-half miles), buses ply between the two parts of the island. During summer, caiques sail to Zoodohos Pigi, a blinding-white monastery whose name means "life-giving springs."

Small, traditional houses to renovate start at $52,000 and you could buy a two-storey house in Poros town for $95,000. A 1,350-square-foot apartment at Askeli is $120,000; a modern house on two levels—it could be divided into two apartments—$184,000. For long-term rentals, expect to pay $225 to $250 monthly for a 770-square-foot apartment.

- **Epenitiki Real Estate,** *Korizi Square, Poros Town, Poros Island, Greece; tel. (30)298-22699 or (30)298-22450; fax (30)298-24280; e-mail: troizina@otenet.gr; website www.ependitiki.com.gr.*

Hydra

The only motorized vehicle on Hydra is a garbage truck. If your own two feet won't get you around, you'll have to use donkey power—there are around 500 on the island.

Primarily beasts of burden, donkeys carry everything from garbage to beer, bottled water supplies to building materials. If you're renting a vacation apartment at the top of one of Hydra's steep stairways and alleys—and some are almost perpendicular—you'll need a donkey to carry your baggage. Each load costs around $15.

Home to 2,500 residents and with just 658 tourist beds, Hydra is one of the Aegean's stars. Strict preservation laws keep it looking the same as in old black-and-white photos. Once a forgotten backwater, it grabbed world attention when Sophia Loren filmed *Boy on A Dolphin* here in 1957.

Since then, Hydra has gained a reputation for exclusivity. Village-style homes (small but habitable) fetch at least $200,000. A small cottage to renovate just sold for $96,300. Vacation properties rent for astounding sums and it's hard finding long-term rentals here. They're like gold dust. Small houses sleeping four in Hydra town rent for at least $145 per night to holiday makers.

Some families live around Kamini, but the island's only real settlement is Hydra town. Classified as a National Monument, it's like an amphitheater with whitewashed houses and exquisitely preserved stone mansions rising in tiers up a cliff face. With their colonnades and balconies, many grander mansions have an almost Venetian look...it was a favorite retreat for wealthy ship owners during the 18th and 19th centuries.

Hydra property sampler

- 645-square-foot, ground-floor apartment, 200 steps up from Hydra harbor. Price: $102,000.

- 860-square-foot apartment in a three-storey stone mansion house with small garden. View to the harbor from bedroom window. Price: $138,000.

- 915-square-foot apartment in immaculate condition in a 200-year-old building 20 steps up from the west corner of Hydra harbor. The agents say it's ideal for those seeking a low-maintenance holiday home and would be easy to rent when you're not using it. Price: $236,400.

- Two-storey house with independent entrances to each level. The property has two living rooms, two bedrooms, two shower rooms, two galley kitchens and a small back courtyard. Described as a good fixer-upper that doesn't need any major structural work, it has 1,000 square feet of living space. Price: $246,500.

- Three-bedroom structurally sound house with huge inner courtyard and spectacular views from its terrace: you can see mountains, valleys, and the sea west of Hydra harbor. Price: $292,800.

- Above Hydra town, a three- to four-bedroom traditional house with 1,400 square feet of living space and lots of character.

One to two living rooms, kitchen, dining room, and sitting room; views of Kamini Valley to the sea, other islands, and the Peloponnese. New roof, new wiring, new plumbing—you could move in tomorrow. Price: $384,000.

Contact for Hydra Island

• **Kelsey Edwards,** *Hydra 180-40, Hydra Island, Greece; tel. (30) 2980-53684; fax (30)2980-53751; e-mail: kelsey@SaronicNet.com; website: www.hydradirect.com.* Ms. Edwards, who is English, has been living on Hydra for the last four years. As well as organizing holiday rentals, she provides space on her website for private property sellers...if title checks out. Don't let the fact that there's no proper address worry you—postmen don't exist on Hydra. Residents must collect their mail from the island's post office.

The Peloponnese—a Greek classic

Can't choose between the dazzle of the sea...and the grandeur of mountains? Then check out the Peloponnese. It's hemmed by azure-blue seas on three sides: the Ionian Sea lies to the west, the Mediterranean to the south, and the Pelagos Sea to the east. Its only link to the mainland is by a massive road and rail bridge over the Corinth Canal.

Covering 8,280 square miles, the region has seven prefectures: Corinthia, Achaia, Elis, Argolis, Arcadia, Laconia, and Messinia. For any initial visit, we'd recommend basing yourself in two centers: Kalamata (Messinia) in the south of the region, and Nafplio (Argolis) in the north.

Dangling like a leaf from the southern Greek mainland, the Peloponnese remains uncrowded and unspoiled. Narrow roads spool down to a dramatically serrated coastline of small crescent coves, sweeping bays and sheltered fishing harbors. The turquoise sea mirrors a skyline of mountain peaks. Snow-capped in winter, the Taygetos soar above a lush and fragrant landscape: a mosaic of pine woods, wildflower meadows, vineyards, olive trees, and citrus groves.

Here classical Greece leaps from the pages of history. Olympia, Mycenae, Sparta, Epidauros, and Mystras are only a tiny fraction of archaeological sites scattered across the region.

Particularly in the south, traditional villages cling like limpets to the mountain slopes. Life carries on has it has done for centuries, pottering by in the slow lane. People make a living from the land and sea rather than tourism. They fish for squid, tend beehives, keep chickens and footloose flocks of goats…then collect their mail from the local kafenion (coffee house) or taverna.

Just about every red-roofed house comes with lemon and olive trees—and most villagers still get their own oil pressed. If you yearn for a simple and affordable life, it's possible to buy simple village houses away from the coast for as little as $54,000.

Prices for seaside plots have doubled in the past year. On average, 11,000-square-foot plots cost $72,000, but similar-sized sites in the hills can still be had for $18,000. An architect-designed stone-built house of one storey costs around $92 per square foot to build.

Messinia: The southern Peloponnese

"The Garden of the Peloponnese," Messinia prefecture has the region's best beaches and some of its most impressive scenery. The "capital" is Kalamata, a seaside resort and port that's home to 55,000 people. A busy commercial city, it has a regional airport and also a yacht marina.

Although much of the city is built in typical concrete block Balkan-style, it has an ancient castle and churches, plus over three miles of white pebble beach. Its seaside setting is spectacular with mountains swooping down to the sea. Around Kalamata's seafront and marina, numerous tavernas and seafood restaurants serve delicious, good value food.

Although most foreign buyers opt for rural homes near to Kalamata rather than a property in the city itself, you might want to buy here. A five-minute's walk from the marina, an apartment with 2,100 square feet of living space and an additional 720 square feet of verandahs is $204,000. It has central heating, solar panels, and parquet and tiled floors throughout. The beach is only 10 minutes away.

West of Kalamata is a string of seaside hamlets and miles of beaches. I recommend you look at historic Pilos, the impressive fortified towns of Koroni and Methoni, and the seaside resort of Finikounda. This part of the Peloponnese is also surrounded by olive groves and rolling mountains. Finikounda village is the star resort for beach lovers and families with young children. Within walking distance are three beaches of coarse pale sand that slope gently into the turquoise sea.

Greco-Immobilien has studio apartments (333 square feet plus terrace) in Finikounda for $54,000, and a two-bedroom house built in 2002 for $156,000. Living space comprises 775 square feet plus terraces and cellar space.

Twin guardians of the Messinian Gulf, the seaside resorts of Koroni and Methoni used to be known as "the eyes of Venice" in the days when the Doges of Venice vied with the French, Spanish—and pirates—for control of southern Europe's seas. Methoni Real Estate mainly sells plots of land there, like a 2,000-square-meter plot with sea view and access to electricity and water for $50,000. Owner Mr. Panagiotis says his architect can build you a house within a year. He also has some resales: a two-storey house of around 1,500 square feet a few miles back from the sea is $93,600.

The Mani

The Peloponnese's central peninsula, the Mani, has a different character. Below the mighty Taygetos mountain range, this is a land where time really does seem to have stopped still. Riven by gorges and festooned with sparkling waterfalls, the northern half (the Outer Mani) is verdant and lush. The southern part (the Inner Mani) feels more like a moonscape. Here the mountains are bare and bleak, and the land— thickly scattered with curious stone towers—is more harsh and barren.

Pretty seaside villages include Aghios Dimitrios, Stoupa (where the dancing-on-the-beach scene in *Zorba the Greek* was filmed) and red-roofed Kardamili. Designated "a village of special beauty," Kardamili is the starting point for some exhilarating hill walking.

Jagged mountains rear up above olive and cypress trees. The pale turquoise sea is as clear as crystal...villages of red-roofed stone houses come straight from an artist's portfolio. Anybody with even half an eye for beauty will be smitten by the extraordinary panorama.

O'Connors agency has a good choice of Mani resales. At Neochori, a village house with its own bread oven is $55,000. Although small (around 750 square feet) and needing about $12,000 worth of refurbishment, it would make a perfect little holiday hideaway. There's a taverna, a *kafenion*, and church almost on the doorstep. During the summer, you could easily charge $400 per week rent...maybe more.

Neochori is a five minute's drive from the sea. Aghios Demetrios is on the coast. Here an architect-designed stone-built house (1,275 square feet) with its own pool and views of both mountains and across the bay to Stoupa is $207,800.

In the hills, Prosilio and Proastio look down on some of the most gorgeous coastal scenery. The village names are just as captivating: they mean "facing the sun" and "facing the stars."

In Prosilio, $99,000 buys two stone houses. The first house of 540 square feet (one room, kitchen, and outside WC/shower), plus courtyard could be used as a cozy holiday home. However, for a modest restoration cost of $18,000, the whole house could be modernized and a bathroom added. Or, if you wished to extend, a traditional Mani tower of 430 square feet could be constructed, adding two bedrooms and a bathroom. A turreted extension like this costs around $43,000. The second cottage is smaller (483 square feet), but could be extended for around $21,000.

The Northern Peloponnese

In the northern Peloponnese, Napflio is one of Greece's prettiest seaside towns. Sheltered by Argolikis Bay, it's a great vacation base for history buffs. Within easy striking distance are two classical biggies: Mycenae and Epidauros.

With views of snow-capped mountains on three sides, and the sea on the other, Napflio's old quarter is a lovely mix of Venetian houses,

Turkish fountains, waterfront fish tavernas, and picturesque back streets and alleyways. Many streets clamber towards one of the town's three Venetian fortresses. Although the town is quiet from Monday to Thursday, it gets busy at weekends. Athenian families come for breaks even in winter.

As it's closer to Athens, house prices and building costs are higher than in the southern Peloponnese. However, it's hard to put a price on homes in Napflio's old town because they rarely surface. Apartments in the modern quarter average $145 per square foot.

For quality residences in nearby resorts, expect to pay around $165 per square foot. Things get a little cheaper in the inland town of Argos, a 20-minute drive from Napflio. Prices in Argos are approximately $135 per square foot and have been rising by around 10% annually.

Unlike in the Mani, Argolid villages are relatively new creations. For anything "traditional," you'll have to look 30 miles or so back in the mountains. The best value lies in villages around 15 minutes from the sea. Plots (5,300 square feet) within the "city plan" and with access to telephone, electricity, and water, cost around $36,000. Construction costs for "middle-class houses" are currently just below $100 per square foot.

East of Nafplio, Tolo is the Argolid coast's largest resort. The cost of land here is far more expensive than in the Argos area. A sea view plot of 5,300 square feet can cost $180,000. That said, if you were looking to rent a place to tourists, you could buy newly built 540-square-foot apartments in Tolo for around $84,000.

Peloponnese property sampler

- Village house to renovate, a 20-minute drive from Kalamata airport. Its floor size is 1,720 square feet and comprises four rooms. There's a small garden too. Price: $42,000.

- With views of olive groves and wildflower meadows, a tiny (590 square feet) hideaway home that's 20 minutes from Pilos. There are only two rooms at present in good condition, but the house can be extended to include up to another 1,600 square feet if you wish. It's on 43,000 square feet of land planted with 100 olive trees. Price: $60,000.

- A 20-minute drive from Pilos, a ready-to-move into village house of 775 square feet in a small fenced-off plot. Central heating has been installed with radiators in all rooms, plus a solar panel for hot water. On one level, it comprises living room, separate kitchen, large bathroom, and two small bedrooms. Price: $70,500.

- A 1,500-square-foot village "house of character." Although needing some restoration, the two-storey house is in good condition with electricity and water connection. Five miles from Koroni on the Gulf of Messinia, the village has mini-markets, a taverna, and sandy beaches less than two miles away. Price: $88,000.

- Just a two-minute drive from a white-sand beach near Koroni, a single-storey 795-square-foot house that has permission for an extension. Otherwise no work is needed. The house stands on a well-kept 1-acre plot with six fig trees and 110 olive trees that would keep you in the world's best olive oil every year. There is an enclosed garden patio with a secluded and shaded leafy BBQ area. Price: $114,600.

- Twenty minutes' drive from the seaside resorts of Pilos and Petalidi, a two-storey house in excellent condition with floor size of 1,935 square feet. Marble floors, central heating, balconies, and garden of 8,600 square feet. Price: $118,000.

- Sea views and garden with orange and lemon trees. A 2,150-square-foot village house with terraces all around, a 30-minute drive from Kalamata and less than two miles from the water's edge. The property could be used as a one-family house or as two separate apartments and rented out. Price: $160,200.

- Forty minutes from Kalamata, and ideal for renting out, a new, three-storey, 1,075-square-foot traditional Mani tower house.

It consists of a combined kitchen and living area, two bedrooms and two to three bathrooms. Price: $193,000.

- On a mountainside overlooking the blue Messinian Gulf, a south-facing house (805 square feet) with additional attic space of 430 square feet that could be used for additional living space. Views range all down the Mani coast and across to Koroni on the opposite peninsula. Outside there is a traditional bread oven and an acre of land planted with 200 fruit trees and 30 olive trees. The plot has its own water and an irrigation system. $204,000.

Contacts for Kalamata

- **O'Connor Real Estate,** *Terma Ethnikou Stadiou, 24100 Kalamata; tel./fax (30)2721-096614; e-mail: oconnor@oconnorproperties.gr; website www.oconnorproperties.gr.*

- **George Maragos Estate Agency,** *1 Danaou St, Argos; tel. (30) 2751-067778; fax (30)2751-023180; e-mail: gmaragos@otenet.gr; website www.greekhouses.gr.*

- **Greco-Immobilien,** *Odos Misirli, Pilos; tel./fax (30)2723-023160 or (30)2723-071020; e-mail: GrecoImmo@aol.com; website www. greco-immobilien.de.*

- **Methoni Real Estate,** *Episkopou Grigoriou, Methoni; tel. (30)2723-031201.*

- **Costas Stamatis,** *4 Sekeri St, Tolo; tel. (30)2752-059100; fax (30)2752-059670.*

What potential buyers should know

Tougher planning laws will be enforced throughout Greece in 2006. Building new homes outside any village or town will be outlawed unless your plot of land comprises a minimum of 8,000 square meters. This will result in much higher prices for land within a settlement's boundary—and resale homes too. Time is running out, so don't leave it too late.

As things stand at the moment, planning permission is usually granted for building on land of 2,000 square meters or less if the plot is situated within the town-planning zone, or fronts a municipal road. For plots outside of the zone, planning permission can be granted if the land is a minimum of 4,000 square meters in size…and there are no forestry or archaeological restrictions.

While Greek island life may sound appealing, it's not going to be just like home. For example, the island of Hydra has to get its water supply shipped in every day—and here storm conditions mean no deliveries of anything. Water sometimes runs out too during summer …and not only on Hydra. Would you feel happy going five days without a shower? Water on all Greek islands is a precious commodity, something foreigners don't always realize.

Island life carries penance as well as all pleasures. Once summer has gone, you may find little to do. Crete stays lively all year round, but on smaller islands many locals leave for Athens in October—and only return for the tourist season.

Here's another thing: the toilet facilities. Like it or not, you cannot put toilet paper into most island toilets. Waste pipes are so narrow that it blocks up the system. What you do is drop your waste toilet paper into plastic bags for collection.

Restrictions

There are some areas of Greece where it's very difficult for foreigners to obtain permission to buy. The Greek Consulate in New York puts out the following information:

"American citizens (of no Greek descent) are able to buy real estate property in Greece except specific regions near the borders of the country, including some of the Greek Islands. The areas (where Americans cannot buy) are as following: Ioannina, Florina, Pella, Serres, Drama, Samos, Chios, Lesvos, Kozani, Kavala, Chalkidiki, Lefkada, Imathia, Thessaloniki, Pieria." However, there are no problems with any of our featured islands—or the Peloponnese.

Buying your home

Although it's unlikely you'll shave any money off the stated price of new property, it's acceptable to make an offer on village houses. How much the vendor will come down is hard to say—it depends how keen they are to sell.

Purchase costs in Greece amount to approximately 10% to 13%. It's difficult to give an exact figure, as "declared values" rarely bear much resemblance to actual values. The taxable (*cadastral*) value of a home can often be one-third to one-half below the true value.

Savings can be made by buying a house or apartment off-plan. Transfer tax is paid only on the tax-assessed value of the plot, bringing total purchase costs down to 7% to 8%.

Purchase Costs
- Purchase tax is levied at 7.24% of the first 12,000 euros ($14,400) of taxable value, and 9.25% on the remainder. A couple purchasing property pays less tax as the first 24,000 euros attracts the 7.24% levy.

- "Union Fees" take 1% of the taxable value up to 44,000 euros ($52,800) and 0.5% on the remainder.

- Lawyers normally charge flat-rate fees of 1,200 to 2,000 euros ($1,440-$2,400) and sometimes take percentages of 1.5% to 2.5%.

- Public notary fee and registration charges are normally 2% of taxable value.

- Agencies charge 2% to 4%.

You must obtain a certification of the property's tax status from the local tax office. This certificate must be attached to the original master copy of the contract held by the public notary.

Putting down a 10% deposit is the norm. A pre-contract is then signed which confirms both parties' details, property description, and any conditions relating to the sale. An appointed lawyer holds the deposit until all searches have been satisfactorily concluded and the sale is authorized.

Incidentally, the vendor of any Greek property must be able to establish title for a minimum of at least 30 years. All title searches must be made manually at the relevant registry. That includes checking volume and folio numbers, all related documentation, etc. These searches must be done by a lawyer. As you might realize, the non-existence of a property registry can make purchasing second-hand homes a Byzantine procedure. The Greek government is in the process of establishing a computerized land-titles registry, but is unlikely to be finished until 2010.

Once the pre-contract is signed, your deposit is non-refundable if you decide against buying. If the seller backs out, your deposit is refunded. Providing the pre-contract states this, the seller must pay you an additional 10% indemnity.

A Public Notary deals with conveyancing documents, and arranges the new title and ownership deed in accordance to Greek law. Prior to signing the final contract, you'll need a Greek tax number, as this must be included in the contract.

Buyers must open a Greek bank account. All transfers for the purchase balance go into this account. It's not necessary to be present to sign documents and make payment—this can be done through power of attorney. Your local lawyer can also pay transfer tax and registration fees on your behalf. The process normally takes three to four weeks.

Obtaining finance

Greek banks are usually reluctant to lend against property to foreign buyers. You will probably be better off trying to arrange finance with an overseas lender.

Residency permits

North Americans don't need visas for visits of less than 90 days. For longer periods, you have to jump through more hoops than citizens of other EU countries. You'll need a residency permit from the Alien's Bureau in Athens. Apply at least two months before your initial three-month stay ends. To be granted a residency permit, you need private health insurance and an adequate pension or income to support yourself. After the Immigration Committee reviews the application, there will be an interview. The Secretary General of the region determines whether a residence permit is granted.

- **Aliens Bureau,** *173 Alexandras Avenue, 11522 Athens; tel. (30) 1-770-5711.*

- **Embassy of Greece,** *2221 Massachusetts Ave NW, Washington, D.C. 20008; tel. (202)939-1318; e-mail: consulate@greekembassy.org.*

Cost of ownership

Annual property taxes are negligible on most properties—usually 20 euros or less—and on some properties you pay nothing at all. However, if the value of a home under joint ownership of a couple exceeds 411,000 euros ($493,000), property tax kicks in at a 0.25% of the declared value. For example, say you buy a house for $500,000 but its declared value is $250,000. Property taxes will then be around $1,250 per year.

In typical new development properties, community fees amount to somewhere in the region of $60 to $70 monthly.

Cost of living

The cost of living is way below that of the United States or northern Europe. A retired couple can enjoy a modest lifestyle on as little as $14,000 per year. Once you've bought or rented a property, day to day living costs are very cheap. Over the course of a year, house maintenance costs plus groceries might be $7,350, dinners for two twice a week $2,600, and car insurance $440.

Two-monthly winter electricity bills average $120. The annual total shouldn't be more than around $520. The breakdown is a standard charge of 135 euro annually plus the usage charge (0.65 euro per kilo-watt, plus 8% VAT). Many homes have solar panels that provide hot water at no charge for eight months of the year.

Electricity bills also include a separate charge for local services such as garbage collection and public street lighting. These services are likely to be in the region of $150 to $180 per year. Annual water rates amount to $160 to $220.

For a telephone, the rental charge is $135 annually plus usage ($0.03 per unit, plus 18% VAT). A unit is equivalent to approximately three minutes.

Central heating is normally oil-based. Estimates are $240 to 300 for annual heating expenses. Fire and theft insurance for a typical two-bedroom home is $300.

It costs around $22 to visit a doctor...it's free, though, to ask the advice of a pharmacist for minor ailments—as many people do. As health insurance is mandatory for non-EU citizens, you can't obtain free hospital treatment—you'll be charged. If you require a major operation or fall seriously ill, you'll probably need to go to Athens.

Groceries are very affordable, particularly fruit and vegetables. Oranges sell for 35 cents a pound. You'll pay around 60 cents for half a dozen eggs, $3.60 for a pound of pork chops or chicken, and $5.40 for a pound of squid. Almost every village has its own bakery, where small loaves cost 95 cents.

Paying your taxes

Income tax rates range from zero to 40%. Permanent residents are taxed on international income, whether earned in Greece or not. If tax has been paid in another country on non-Greek income, the double-taxation treaty ensures against paying tax twice.

Temporary residents are taxed only on income earned in Greece. But even if planning to buy a home solely for vacations, any funds brought into Greece need declaring. It's done by opening a Greek bank account and transferring funds from your home bank. This ensures they're properly registered and thus not liable for tax. You'll receive a "Pink Slip" receipt for these imported amounts. Keep them all. Home owners must complete annual tax declaration forms, and employ an accountant.

The tax system in a nutshell
* Tax is only liable on amounts exceeding an annual income of 10,000 euro ($12,000).

* Income exceeding the basic amount by up to 3,400 euro (that is, total income of up to 13,400 euros or $16,000) is levied at 15%. However, only the amount exceeding the based level is taxed at the higher rate, not the whole.

* Income exceeding the basic amount by up to 13,400 euro (that is, total income of up to 23,400 euro or $28,000) is taxed at 30%.

* Income greater than 23,400 euro ($28,000) is taxed at 40%.

When you come to sell

You will be exempt from capital gains tax if the proceeds from the sale of a home are going toward the purchase of another property in Greece. Otherwise it will be between 10% and 25%, depending on how long the property has been owned.

Chapter 4

Italy

Hills crowned by flawlessly preserved walled towns glowing in warm shades of pink, ochre, and gold. A verdant countryside of vineyards and medieval castles, of olive groves and stone farmhouses. A glittering silvery blue sea and endless miles of beaches. Fabulous food and wine. The "wallowing in a libretto" landscape of the Italian Lakes. Rome, Venice, Milan, and Florence, the world's greatest art city...

Italy's appeal is timeless and you certainly don't have to pay crazy sums for homes. Much depends on where you look. In countless picture-perfect villages, medieval houses to restore start from as little as $45,000.

An apartment? Same again—much depends on where you look. Whereas you'll pay almost $650,000 for 1,050 square feet of living space in Florence's best areas, the same amount of space only costs a sixth of the price in the delightful Umbrian hill town of Norcia. What's more, you'll be living in a genuine—but restored—medieval palace.

A romantic *casa colonica* farmhouse? While they do trade hands for $1 million and more in the best-known parts of central and southern Tuscany, the price falls to around $160 to $185 per square foot—sometimes less—for fully restored properties in northern Tuscany, Umbria, and Le Marche.

Take this one: a small but classic *casa colonica* of natural pink stone with 21,000 square feet of land planted with pine, cypress, olive trees, and a small vineyard. It doesn't need a great deal of work...the hilltop setting is dreamy: open green meadows, bosky thickets, and scattered farms...in the distance, a picturesque village whose stone houses snuggle into a steep slope. It's a 30-minute drive from sandy beaches. Price: $177,000.

City options

It's impossible to give an average price for Italy as a whole, though most properties range from $2,000 to $3,360 per square meter (or $186 to $313 per square foot). As a rule of thumb, you'll pay far less for apartments in provincial towns than in major population centers.

Sometimes a lot less. The price of an apartment in Tarquinia, a small city in Lazio province 90 minutes from Rome, is $119,000 for 965 square feet—about $125 per square foot. The apartment is in an 18th-century courtyard building that used to be the residence of the Bruschi Falgari counts. While the unit needs updating, the building has no structural problems and was renovated recently. For more information, contact the Britain-based **European Property Network**, *tel. (44)1425-654671; website: www.europropertynet.com.*

Within each city, price variations can be enormous. Overall, Venice is costliest for homes, but the average price of a 1,075-square-foot apartment in prime areas of Florence is now nudging towards $650,000.

In southern Italy, the average local buyer is looking for a home at $145,000. In wealthier north and central Italy, the average amount spent is $265,000. This "average" encompasses everything from poky studios to flash villas. In the apartment market, square-foot prices can be as low as $45 in the sleazier back streets of Bari but as high as $1,120 to overlook the Trevi fountain in Rome.

Average square-foot prices in selected Italian cities
Venice—$410 to $895 and up.
Milan—$615 to $725 in central Milan, up to $820 around via Spigia and the fashion district.
Rome—$235 to $1,120 and up.
Florence—$235 to $615.
San Remo (Italian Riviera)—$225 to $445.
Palermo (Sicily)—$90 to $235.
Western Liguria—beyond the Riviera

Linking Tuscany with France is the highly sought-after golden crescent of coastline known as the Italian Riviera, part of Liguria province.

On the coast at Santa Margherita di Ligure, you'll pay $780 to $895 per square foot for frontline beach apartments, and $445 to $560 per square foot in the town center. Yes...here you can pay $895,000 for a 1,000-square-foot apartment. Villas here are equally expensive...a 1,600-square-foot property costs at least $1 million.

But you can buy in Liguria for less than $16,000. High above the beach umbrellas perches a part of the province that tourists seldom see. Smothered in olive trees and vineyards, the Ligurian hinterland mirrors Tuscany with its small, romantic hill towns. Their cobbled streets and tiny squares were designed for mule traffic, not Fiats. In most places you'll have to leave your car on the edge of town...you cannot take it into a town or village's historic center.

Of course, no traffic only adds to the ambience. And the *ambiente* really is something special. Homes have high-vaulted ceilings...churches brim with paintings and frescoes...age-old fairs and festivals abound. You'll also discover a mouth-watering array of small *trattorie*. And though many villages are less than 40 minutes from the Mediterranean, prices are astoundingly cheap.

If you're looking for property to renovate, you'll be pleased to know that western Liguria has dozens of traditional village houses still waiting to be snapped up—many for under $50,000. They can be as low as 13,000 euro ($15,600). That's the asking price of a small stone house at Andagna, a medieval hilltop village 16 miles from the coast. Naturally at that price it needs total restoration!

Time seems to stand still in villages like Triora, Borgomaro, Apricale, Ceriana, and Corte— all particularly good hunting grounds for bargains. On holy days, torchlight processions still wind through the narrow streets of Glori to the sanctuary of Madonna di Lourdes in the chestnut woods. Just $16,800 is the price of another tiny stone house to renovate here.

Small houses you could move straight into start at $84,000. Casa Antica has one at that price at Colle San Bartolomeo. At Argallo, $102,000 buys a renovated stone house (915 square feet) on 43,000 square feet of land with panoramic views—and it's just 30 minutes drive from the sea.

Finally, remember we mentioned those $1 million villas in Santa Margherita? At Trioria, you can buy a six-bedroom, two-bathroom villa with terraces and a small garden for $198,000.

- **Casa Antica, Piazza dei Carri,** *18010 Molina di Triora, Liguria; tel. (39)1849-4633; e-mail: info@casaantica.com; website: www.casa antica.com.*

Tuscany

Tuscany is the best-known region of Italy's Renaissance heartland. The landscape is mesmerizing—straight from the canvas of one of those *quattrocento* paintings by the great Italian masters. Bathed in golden light, dreamy hilltop villages tower above seas of yellow sunflowers. Columns of cypress trees stand like sentinel guards on the horizon. Steeped in centuries of history, its towns are like backdrop images from a Book of Hours—a bejeweled mirage of bell towers, churches, and palaces all glowing in warm, antique colors.

But, Tuscany has a frightening reputation for costly properties. And if you stick to the countryside around Florence and Siena, you'll discover that its reputation is well-deserved. The "Golden Triangle" has been so long sought after, even heaps of farmhouse rubble usually cost $250,000 and upwards.

Yet you can have Tuscany at a sensible price—if you look to Lunigiana. This almost unknown sliver of idyllic countryside is in the region's northwestern-most tip, about an hour from Pisa airport.

So far, very few foreigners have discovered its castles, country churches, and clusters of walled villages. But it's only a matter of time before word gets out that small stone-built village houses in habitable condition still pop up for $48,000 to $60,000.

While you'd probably spend another $36,000 on modernizing a typical $60,000 village house (plumbing and electricals are unlikely to meet the average buyer's approval), these houses have not fallen into rack and ruin. They're sound homes, not wrecks.

Although Lunigiana has the hallmarks of a secret land, it's only a half-hour drive from the Ligurian seaport city of La Spezia. And La Spezia itself is only a hop, skip, and a jump away from Ligurian beauty spots such as the Gulf of Poets and the Cinque Terre's painted fishing villages. Owning a home in this corner of Tuscany means seaside pleasures are on your doorstep...but you're not penalized by coastal prices.

Good condition village houses are plentifully available for $108,000 to $180,000. Take this bargain: a restored stone house (1,250 square feet) with courtyard in Tavernelle village. It has three bedrooms, two bathrooms, and fitted kitchen with terracotta tiled floors. A real 16th-century beauty. It's $144,000 and you could move straight in.

In Catognano village, $110,000 currently buys a 1,400-square-foot house with decent roof, beamed ceilings, and great views down the wooded valley. Although habitable, the house would benefit from having an additional $20,000 to $45,000 spent on modernization. "Strip off the pine-cladding, put down terracotta tiles, redo the wiring, and you'd have a lovely home," says agent Lois Allan. "Good tiles in particular always transform a property."

A castle? You can have one for $420,000—and it's no wreck. The old lady owner is only now in the process of moving out. The local doctor also had his office in the castle until recently. With eight habitable rooms downstairs, and the possibility of creating another 15 rooms on its upper floor, the back of the castle dates from the 13th century and the front from the 16th. It's on the main square of a village called Licciana Nardi. Next door is the church—and although it's now blocked off, an enclosed bridge-like passageway once connected the two buildings.

Licciana Nardi's mayor hopes the castle's buyer will turn it into a small hotel. Although no demesne comes with it, a half-acre vineyard is included in the price. However, it needs stressing that Italian castles don't normally feature towers and turrets. They were constructed to suggest brute strength and power—aesthetic beauty didn't figure in the plans.

Few opportunities exist to buy building land and construct new. As elsewhere in Tuscany, Lunigiana is a green zone, which means building regulations are very tough. For example, you cannot knock down a single-storey farmhouse and build a three-storey modern villa on the site…or transform a shepherd's cottage into something more suited to the lord of the manor. However, if you do buy a property with land attached, there doesn't seem to be any difficulty in getting permission for a swimming pool—starting price is $18,000 for a small one.

Another part of Tuscany worth investigating is around the hill town of Cortona, not far from the Umbrian border. Built on an Etruscan settlement, Cortona holds many cultural events throughout the year including a medieval archery contest, a *fungi porcini* mushroom festival, operas, antique fairs…and…an outdoor cinema in the public gardens in the summer. European Property Network has a fully restored 750-square-foot apartment on the top two floors of an ancient building in the upper part of Cortona's medieval town for $189,000. During the restoration of the apartment, care was taken to maintain all original features including a stone fireplace, terracotta floor tiles, beamed ceilings, and some beautiful old-fashioned doors.

- **Immobiliare L'Architrave** (Lois Allan), *Piazza Giarella 4, Monti, Licciana Nardi 54017 MS, Italy; tel. (39)1874-72068; e-mail: loallan@tin.it; website www.larchitrave.it.*

Umbria

Umbria is Tuscany's next-door-neighbor. Nicknamed the "Green Heart of Italy," it shares the same dramatic "Cradle of the Renaissance" landscapes. Billowing out beyond the jumble of russet-roofed houses jumbled here and there are league upon league of bosky hills. The panorama of woods and olive groves and little stone hamlets seems to go on forever. Buy a honey-hued stone home in one of these small villages and you'll enjoy views of towns gleaming like tiaras on their green mounds.

Perugia, the regional capital, has some magnificent cultural treasures… a prestigious university for foreigners…and a summer jazz festival for which the town becomes a citadel of music. Like most of Umbria's settlements, it has a medieval core of alleys and archways and a history going back beyond Roman times to the Etruscans.

All palaces, turrets, and spiky battlements, countless smaller towns are rich in medieval splendors: Spoleto, Gubbio, Orvieto, and Assisi—birthplace of St Francis. Then there's Todi. Some years ago, researchers from Kentucky University declared it "the most livable town in the world." Within its walls, Piazza del Popolo vies for the title of Italy's most perfect medieval piazza.

Driving 16 miles from Todi, on the square of Quadrelli village, Casaitalia has a perfectly restored. 1,450-square-foot house called La Portella for $282,000. It's named for the gate that used to give access to the village during the Middle Ages. On three levels, with timbered ceilings and terracotta tiles, the house has a typically medieval structure —planned vertically like the region's ancient tower houses. The ground floor, once a tavern, has a wide stone arch dividing the entrance from the living room.

Umbria is second only to Tuscany in popularity with expats seeking farmhouses, so bargains take some unearthing. Local agents say the countryside—like neighboring Montepulciano (a classic Tuscan wine-growing area)—offers substantially reduced prices. But don't expect pocket-money prices for the rural properties. On 25 acres, a farmhouse and annex to be restored (again, just a ruin) is $252,000. A 30-year-old house in move-into condition with 1 acre is $498,000.

But does it have to be a farmhouse? An Umbrian village only eight miles from the Tuscan border, Citta della Pieve, is an undiscovered treasure. Home to just 6,000 people, it features historic rose-brick buildings and dazzling views. The village overlooks the Valley of Chiana and Lago di Trasimeno, Italy's fourth-largest lake. An apartment of 770 square feet is on the market for $138,000. In the lakeside town of Castiglione del Lago, the average rate for apartments and small houses is $125 per square foot.

Deeper into Umbria is the ravishing hill town of Spoleto. "The most romantic city I ever saw," gushed the English poet Percy Shelley. There's much to gush about: Spoleto rises from the wooded countryside like something from a dream. Girdled by pre-Roman walls and complete with a medieval aqueduct, its steep labyrinthine streets lead past Renaissance palaces, Romanesque churches, and a Roman theater.

Not that Spoleto is trapped in a time warp. There's a modern quarter below the archways of the *centro storico*—where you'll find realtor's offices. Adolfo Giovannelli of CasaItalia says restored *casa coloniche* in the surrounding countryside average $170 per square foot. Doing the math, you can expect to pay around $425,000 for a decent-sized farmhouse you could immediately call home.

Other options are available: a fairly modern home, a 15-minute drive from Spoleto, costs $464,000. It has 2,100 square feet of living space and 12.5 acres planted with olive trees.

Then there's the Palazzo Tebaldeschi, a restored old palace, in a small town called Norcia. Apartments of around 1,050 square feet start at $120,000. In Trevi, another tiara-like hill town, CasaItalia has a 3,200-square-foot apartment in another restored 16th century palace for $264,000.

One of their most stunning properties is in the ancient fortified hamlet of Labro, which dates back to the 10th century. On the border between Umbria and Lazio, the village features twisted alleyways, ancient doors, arches, and stone stairways. In the highest part of the center of the village, Casa Le Scalette is a perfectly restored ancient jewel of a dwelling with private roof garden and terraces giving stupendous views over Labro to the green hills beyond. Although the total surface area is a medieval 1,000 square feet, two mezzanine bedrooms give the impression that it's more spacious. The price is $312,000.

- **Epoch Villas/Studio Tecnico** (Marino Miscio and Francesco Sacco), *via P. Vannucci 39, 06062 Citta della Pieve; tel. (39)578-298497; fax (39)348-2282196.*

- **Casa Italia** (Adolfo Giovannelli), *Piazza della Vittoria 26, 06049 Spoleto; tel. (39)743-220122; e-mail: info@casait.it; website www.casait.it.* (This agency also has properties in Tuscany, Le Marche, and Sardinia.)

Le Marche

Le Marche is a part of central Italy practically unknown to foreign travelers...and home buyers. Pronounced "Lay Markay," its name means the *marches,* border country. This is where Italy's Renaissance landscapes skirt the hot southern provinces of the *Mezzogiorno,* the realms of the midday sun.

The tranquil countryside is sublime, a symphony of monasteries and small towns embedded in the folds of green hills. It looks like the crumpled-up bedspread of a storybook giant. "Italy all in one region," says the local tourist board—and they're right. Hill towns, beaches, mountains, art treasures, summer opera festivals...all the things that entice us to Italy meld together here.

Medieval towns like Urbino and Jesi can easily match more famous Tuscan locations for beauty. Nine miles from Urbino, Eurocasa has a small farmhouse to restore in a nice position with valley views. The house is built in local stone and will convert to living space of around 2,150 square feet. The property includes 54,000 square feet of land and is listed at $90,000.

Indicating how much renovated farmhouses can be worth, the same agency has a fully restored farmhouse in a mountainous area close to the border with Umbria. Presently divided into three separate apartments, it's listed at $372,000.

In the south of the province, near Macerata and the Sibellini mountains, European Property Network has a recently restored apartment (750 square feet) in an old monastery that dates back to 1650. One of a complex of apartments, it's in the historic center of the village of Sant' Angelo in Pontano. Price is $79,000.

The Marche region is lapped by the Adriatic, its coastline strung with little resorts where Italians (not foreigners) spend vacations under brightly colored beach ombrellones. A working town as well as a summer resort, San Benedetto del Tronto is famed for its 7,000 palm trees. Attractive beaches, a long promenade, lively center, and enough palm trees to merit the title Riviera del Palme.

As in most of Le Marche's seaside towns, homes here range from new constructions to ancient aristocratic mansions and Liberty-style villas. One-bedroom apartments start at around $60,000. A three-bedroom duplex apartment in a piccola palazzina—an authentic little palace—is $192,000.

- **Italian Countryside Estates** (Andrea Cristofanelli Broglio); *e-mail: andcb@tin.it; website www.marchecountry.it.*

- **Gabetti** (Cristina Rosi), *Viale della Vittoria 93E; 60035 Jesi (AN); tel. (39)731-57092; fax (39)731-57076; e-mail: gabetti.jesi@ tascalinet.it; website www.gabetti.it.*

- **Eurocasa** (Maria Cristina Marchetti), *via Mazzini 37, 61029 Urbino (PS); tel./fax (39)722-339179; e-mail: info@eurocasaonline.it; website www.eurocasaonline.it.*

The northern lakes

Italy's northern lakes form a natural gateway to the hot, languorous south. Within an hour's journey of Milan—one of Europe's best shopping cities—there is a quartet of lakes to consider: Como, Lugano, Maggiore, and Garda.

Crowned with ancient churches whose sonorous bells summon the faithful to early evening mass, most lakeside villages are storybook affairs...exquisite toytowns straight from an operetta. Cobbled streets clamber precariously up towards forested hills, and sparkling waterfalls descend into little rivers spanned by arched stone bridges. Draped in bougainvillea and wisteria, village houses are painted in warm summer shades of daffodil, peach, pink cream, and butterscotch; their perfumed gardens brimming with palm trees, statuary, late-flowering roses, and all kinds of tropical flowers.

Dotted between the waterfront settlements are sumptuous Renaissance villas—some restored to their former glory, others remaining draped in an almost gothic melancholy. Admiring the faded elegance of these palatial residences—all moss-covered stone belvederes and lush gardens descending in terraces down to the shore—you get the impression that the passage of time has made little impact at all.

Antique villas are expensive, mostly pitched between $270,000 and $2 million...and at the lower end of the scale you're buying a restoration project. One restored villa in *perfette condizioni* with garden that's currently on the market in Stresa (Lake Maggiore) is $480,000. It's fairly sizeable, too, with 2,360 square feet of living space.

However, if you're willing to share your baroque or Belle Epoque residence, it's possible to find something more affordable. Not all villas are individually owned—a number have been divided into apartments. For example, an apartment (700 square feet) in a restored *palazzina* in Stresa could be yours for $132,000. A modern home (1,400 square feet) with lake views in the Maggiore lakeside village of Baveno (a favorite of Queen Victoria's) is $336,000.

Casa Travella, based in Britain, has apartments in a new residence with pool at Montemezzo, at Lake Como's northern end. Prices are from $126,000 to $162,000. Every apartment has a lake view—some more and some less, reflected in the price. All properties have two bedrooms, two bathrooms, living room, kitchen, car space, and either balcony or garden. The residence is 16 miles from Madesimo's ski slopes. Como Town is 36 miles away and the Milan airport is about one-and-a-quarter hours away by car.

- **Habitat & Domina Stresa,** *Via Roma 16, 28838 Stresa (VB); tel. (39)323-31014 or (39)323-934-025; e-mail: info@hdstresa.com; website www.hdstresa.com.*

- **Casa Travella Ltd.,** *65 Birchwood Road, Wilmington, Kent DA2 7HF, United Kingdom; tel. (44)1322-660-988; e-mail: casa@travella. f9.co.uk; website www.casatravella.com.*

Sardinia

A scented island of soaring mountain pinnacles, Sardinia belongs to Italy. The 800-mile-long coastline is studded with amazing granite rock formations, the turquoise sea is as crystal clear as a looking glass, and you still come across villages where clocks seem to have stopped a couple of hundred years ago.

Aside from in larger cities, you don't see any ugly high-rises. All along the coastline, villas and apartment houses are attractive, stylish, and colorful. Not sugary or garish colors, but lovely soft pinks, golds, ochre, and pale blues. Sardinians are environmentally conscious: all new buildings have to be painted in shades that mirror the natural surroundings

Plenty of Italians come for summer vacations, but most other nationalities ignore Sardinia. That's undoubtedly because there are huge misconceptions about the island. The main one is that properties sell for crazy sums, and thus it's unrealistic for ordinary mortals to consider buying. That's not true. Yes, on one part of the island (the Costa Smeralda) the plushest villas come to market with $20-million price tags. However, elsewhere on Sardinia, you can find properties costing far less than that.

Extending from Portobello to the Costa Smeralda's western boundary is Gallura, Sardinia's northernmost tip. Breathtaking views are everywhere. One moment you're gazing upon the islands of the Maddalena Archipelago; the next it's the white cliffs of the citadel town of Bonifacio in Corsica.

Artists love this region of spiky granite mountains, giant tombs, and curious seashore rock formations...one near Cannigione looks exactly like a bear. The shallow water goes from palest aquamarine to deepest turquoise. The beaches are splendid...ribbons of soft white sand.

Part of Gallura, the resort village of Palau has lovely beaches, sparkling seas rippling through every gradient of turquoise, and ferries over to Maddalena Island. Umbrian agents at Casa Italia are marketing a new low-rise residential development at Palau's Vecchio Marina with views towards the Maddalena archipelago. Houses and apartments are very pretty, painted sunrise pink and yellow. One-bedroom units (530 square feet plus terrace) are from $164,000; two-bedroom units (750 square feet plus terrace) start at $208,000 and villas (1,135 square feet) with private gardens and 435 square feet of terraces begin at $346,000. Prices seem reasonable considering it's only a 20-minute drive to the famous Costa Smeralda where the entry point is around $2 million for villas.

Casa Italia offers to manage these Palau properties as seasonal rentals. They say returns of up to 8% can be achieved. The agency also has apartments in Porto Cervo on the Costa Smeralda, but the cheapest one-bedroom apartment is $402,000. (Why is the Costa Smeralda so expensive? Because it was designed by the Aga Khan as an enclave for the rich and famous—and it bears no resemblance to the real Sardinia.)

South of the Costa Smeralda, Casa Italia is also marketing properties at Residence Bellevue. Ten minutes away from the town of Olbia, on the Gulf of Aranci, this complex of apartments and villas opens onto three miles of fine, white-sand beach. Two-bedroom garden apartments (712 square feet) start at $120,000; detached villas are from $372,000 to $590,000.

How much to restore a farmhouse?

Farmhouses are often completely derelict...way beyond normal renovation. Even for $250,000, many aren't even salvageable. You'd need to demolish and build from scratch...install water, electricity, plumbing...often put in an access road, too.

Is buying such a property just for the foolhardy? Not necessarily. With planning permission difficult to get for new building, the fact that a dwelling is already there means you shouldn't encounter problems in getting permission to build a habitable home.

Another point. Prices also depend on how much acreage comes with the property....whether it has a vineyard...olive groves...or set-aside farmland for which the EU bestows subsidies for leaving pastures fallow.

Having an olive grove on your property sounds appealing, but it bumps up prices tremendously. For example, 39 Tuscan acres planted with 730 olive trees are on the market right now. These trees yield around 12,000 kilos of olives which in turn produce 2,000 kilos of extra-virgin olive oil. This plot is priced at $247,000, which translates to well over $6,000 per acre. Apart from an outbuilding, there's no house with this land at all.

Taking into account whether complete demolition is required, materials used, and local labor costs, restoring a ruined farmhouse is likely to be somewhere between $70 to $120 per square foot. On average, small to medium-sized farmhouses are 2,500 to 3,500 square feet in size. So, you've parted with $400,000 for a 3,500-square-foot pile of prime Tuscan rubble...one with a few acres and a clutch of olive trees in the Siena vicinity.

In this part of Tuscany, it can take almost two years to get onto the list of a reputable builder. Let's say you've been given a price of $85 per square foot to restore the property. 3,500 x 85 = $297,500. That's nudging $700,000 in total...and you haven't even installed your $30,000 swimming pool yet! Or put in an access road...which will cost around $50,000. And if you want your new casa colonica to resemble something from a color supplement—all marble bathrooms and a Jacuzzi—you'll pay even more.

In contrast, ruined farmhouses in parts of the Lunigiana region of Tuscany, over the mountains in the province of Emilia-Romagna and in some corners of Le Marche, still surface for under $80,000. Here you're unlikely to wait longer than six months to get a good builder...and labor costs are cheaper, too. Builders charge around $27 an hour; their assistant gets paid about half that. During a trip to Le Marche, I saw a habitable farmhouse for $162,000 in the Fossombrone area. Only needing modernizing rather than major restoration, renovation costs were estimated at $25,000.

Finding a real estate agent

Italian sales and rental agents are called *immobiliari* and almost 6,500 of them belong to FIAIP (Federazione Italiana Agenti Immobiliari Professionali). Contact the federation for names and addresses of agents in your chosen area or check out the group's website at *www.fiaip.net*. The website lists all agents who are members and lists a few individual agencies too.

- **FIAIP**, *Sede Nazionale Via Monte Zebio 30, Rome 00195; tel. (39)6321-9798; e-mail: info@fiaip.it.*

- In Florence: **Milligan & Milligan**, Carol Milligan, *Via Alfani*

68-50121, Florence, Italy; tel. (39)55-268-256; fax (39)55-268-260; website: www.Italy-Rentals.com, e-mail: Italy@InternationalLiving.com.

Renting property

Monthly rentals for furnished property can be as low as $540 to $600 in Italy's deep south, but the norm in most provincial towns is $750 to $1300 for 1,000 to 1,200 square feet. It can be a lot more in major cities, though. Here's some samples of current rental properties. Agents normally charge a month's rent in commission fees.

Rental prices in selected Italian cities
- Milan (central)—880-square-foot apartments, good condition, $950 to $1,500 monthly.

- Rome—660-square-foot apartment, $900 to $1,370.

- Bologna—880 square feet, $1,050 to $1,275.

- Florence—from $800 for studios and one bedrooms; two-bed room furnished apartment in San Spirito, fourth floor walkup, $1,800. Three-bedroom apartment, $2,250.

- Lake Garda—fully furnished three-bedroom, three-bathroom apartment with terrace overlooking the lake; swimming pool and spa bath; 40 minutes from Verona, $2,400.

What potential buyers should know

Like in other European countries, Italy has no multiple listings system. Each agent has his or her own little cache of properties, so a lot of legwork is involved.

It's estimated that only 10% of Italian agents speak English...and this is what we found on our own travels throughout Italy. All the agents listed in this chapter speak English—and they're professionals.

One important warning if you decide to investigate. There are some rogues out there—both Italian and expatriate—selling over-priced properties. Their main areas of operation are Tuscany and Umbria, and their target market seems to be poorly informed Americans. While prices in Italy are always negotiable, most buyers expect to negotiate downwards...not upwards.

The vacation rental market is a huge money spinner for the unscrupulous, too. Apparently those with more money than sense willingly pay up to $40,000 a week to rent a Tuscan property during summer. Yes, $40,000 a week!

Restrictions

There are no restrictions on foreigners buying property in Italy.

Buying your home

Once an offer has been accepted, a *compromesso di vendita* is drawn up. This document contains details of the price agreed, the deposit paid, the date by which completion will take place, the name of the *notaio* (notary) who will execute the deeds (the *rogito*), and all the terms and conditions of the sale. The deposit is generally 15% to 20% of the agreed price.

In general, on second homes, you should estimate an additional 15% to cover purchase costs and fees for your lawyer, notary, and real estate agent. Additional purchase costs can actually be as low as 12%— or as high as 19% of the value of the property. This variation exists because of the wide range of tax rates applicable to house and land transactions.

The amount payable depends on whether the property is your only home or a second home...whether it's a new home...whether you are a resident. Registration tax (stamp duty) is usually 10% of a property's declared value for second homes and 4% if it is your main home.

An idiosyncrasy of buying in Italy is that this tax is calculated using official tables based on declared value of the property—not the actual purchase price. The declared value is based on official calculations made by the Land Registry. It can be as much as 50% less than the actual price you've paid.

Regarding new property, value added tax (IVA) is levied at 10% on non-luxury properties and 20% on luxury properties defined as such in the property register. However, IVA is normally included in the price charged by the builder or developer. Those who build their own home pay a reduced rate of IVA at 4%.

Notary fees are around 3% of the declared value of the property. He or she checks documents recorded at the Land Registry that may affect title, and also ensures there are no debts against the property. It's the notary's job to register the new title with the Property Registry and deposit the deeds with the relevant authorities.

Sellers usually pay agency fees of 3% to 5% of the purchase price. Like many agencies who target the English-speaking market, L'Architrave in the Lunigiana charge 5%. Their fee includes viewing service, drawing up the *compromesso di vendita* in dual language, conveyance, and preparation of the documentation required for completion, translations, and transfer of utilities.

Obtaining finance

Italy's mortgage industry is still in its infancy compared to other European countries, and foreigners find it fairly difficult to obtain finance. You may be better contacting one of the overseas lenders who have recently moved into Italy. One is the British bank and mortgage lender, Abbey National. They have opened branches all over Italy, and mortgage advisers are bilingual.

For non-resident applicants, Abbey National has a loan-to-value ratio that differs than that for residents. For non-EU buyers, the maximum amount they'll lend is 50% of the price of a property. However, if you intend to live full time in Italy—and apply for and receive residency—the bank's policy governing residents will apply. You may be able to get a mortgage of 75%, possibly more.

Unfortunately you will not be able to get an Abbey National loan (*www.abbeynational.it*) for a fixer-upper property. The property must be certified as residential. (Rural homes newly certified as residential are acceptable.) It must be in habitable condition without requiring improvement and not be isolated. The valuation carried out by Abbey's surveyor must confirm the normal marketability of the property.

With German lenders BHW (*www.bhw.de*), you could obtain up to 75% of the value for the purchase or building (or both) of a house. They also give up to 100% for restoration works. BHW loans can be from five to 30 years. Borrowers must be 18 years or older with the period of loan end before the applicant's 75th birthday. However, the loan contract is in Italian. If you are unable to read and write Italian, a court-approved interpreter is required. One alternative is to provide a "proxy power of attorney" to a person who reads and writes Italian. This proxy power of attorney must be issued by the Italian Embassy in your country.

Residency permits

North American citizens, traveling as tourists, don't need visas to stay in Italy for up to 90 days. If you intend staying for a longer period, you must obtain a long-stay visa from an Italian consulate before you leave home.

Within eight days of arrival, you then have to contact the local police authority (*questura*) to obtain a residence permit (*permesso di soggiorno*) which is the only document that legitimizes the stay of a foreign citizen in Italian territory. Without this permit, you cannot sign contracts with utility and telephone companies or open a bank account. For more information, contact the Embassy of Italy in your home country.

- **Embassy of Italy,** *1601 Fuller St, NW, Washington, D.C. 20009, U.S.; tel. (202)328-5500; fax (202)462-3605.*

The cost of owning property

Annual property taxes amount to 0.4% to 0.7%. For a property valued at $150,000, they would be around $750.

Known as spese in Italian, these are general expenses for apartment dwellers. The average is around $1,500 per year. However, we came across one apartment in Milan where the annual charges were a massive $13,000.

You also have to pay ICI taxes, a local authority charge that pays for trash collection. This tax is around $180 annually. Insurance premiums for a typical apartment will cost around $250 annually.

The cost of living

Italy isn't Europe's cheapest country. In addition to rental costs, an aspiring single expatriate will need an annual income of between $20,000 and $25,000 to live a middle-class lifestyle—run a car, eat out, visit the opera, and go to soccer matches. A couple will probably require $25,000 to $40,000. (However, we do know of one American girl in Rome who reckons she can manage on $16,000 a year.)

Annual electricity bills generally amount to around $1,200 for a family, though it's likely to be somewhat higher during the winter if you decide not to use any gas...and if you choose to live in one of Italy's alpine regions.

More cost-efficient than electricity, gas can be used for both cooking and heating. If you buy or rent an apartment, you may find that the system is centralized and the supply is part of the spese (general expenses) shared by all occupants of the building. Of course, it can be independent too, and therefore paid according to consumption. Depending on the size of the property and whether you live in the north or south, annual costs for cooking and heating are likely to be in the region of $1,500 to $2,200.

Water charges are generally included in service charges for apartment dwellings, but individual homes are on a metered supply controlled by the local municipality. Charges vary, but are normally between 77 cents and $1.90 per cubic meter.

Telephone connection costs $144; line rental is currently $208 annually. Through Interurbane, local calls cost $0.025 a minute cheap rate and $0.05 at peak time. A three-minute call to the U.S. with Telefonica is 61 cents. If you need Internet access, there are free ISPs. You can rent an ISDN line for $24 monthly.

The cost of a routine visit to private doctor is approximately $70.

Americans can join the Italian national health plan. The premium is determined according to the principal applicant's worldwide income at a rate of 7.5%. It cannot be less than the equivalent $465.

In a simple back-street trattoria, you can have a plate of spaghetti and mussels washed down with a small jug of house wine for around $11. Grandstand locations cost more, particularly in northern Italy. A couple can easily spend $70 to $90 on a three-course dinner and a bottle of Bardolino or Chianti wine.

Paying your taxes

Personal income tax (IRPEF) applies to income derived from sources such as employment, self-employment, income from real estate, etc. After allowances have been taken into account, rates are on a sliding scale: 18.5% for amounts up to approximately $11,000; 25.5% for the next band up to $15,500; 33.5% for amounts between $15,500 and $31,000; 39.5% for amounts between $31,000 and $70,000; and 45.5% for amounts over $70,000.

Resident individuals are liable for IRPEF on their worldwide income. Non-resident individuals are subject to IRPEF only on income arising from Italian sources. For income-tax purposes, individuals are considered resident if their habitual abode is in Italy, the center of their interests is in Italy, and they are registered as resident for the greater part of the tax period in public records.

When you decide to sell

Italy recently abolished its inheritance tax and greatly curtailed the gift tax. All investment income and capital gains are now taxed at a slim 12.5%.

Chapter 5

Malta and Gozo

From the air, the Maltese archipelago resembles tiny stepping stones that some ancient god scattered across the Mediterranean. Since antiquity, these outposts have served as a bridge linking southern Italy to North Africa—and Western Europe to the Middle East. They were inhabited way before St. Paul was shipwrecked on Malta's western shore and early Christians burrowed under sun-baked rocks to build catacombs for their dead.

Lying south of Sicily, a quintet of sunny islands makes up the Republic of Malta. Malta, Gozo, and Comino are all inhabited...though with a mere handful of families, Comino only just qualifies. The remaining islands, Cominotto and Filfla, are for boat-trippers and seabirds.

Lapped by translucent crystal waters, Malta and Gozo are both treasure islands. Ancient cities of golden stone...megalithic monuments...fertility goddesses known as Fat Ladies...the Knights of Malta...natural harbors crammed with gleaming white yachts and tiny *luzzu* fishing smacks painted in vibrant colors of red, blue, and yellow. Many depict the Eye of Osiris, a charm dating from the days when the Phoenicians ruled the islands. The "eye" provides protection from the perils of the deep.

On both Malta and Gozo, the living is easy and affordable. Crime hardly exists, the locals are hospitable, permanent foreign residents can take advantage of a 15% tax rate, and nobody pays property taxes. And you'll encounter no language difficulties...everybody speaks English.

Plus, the Maltese islands have fair-weather, averaging 5.2 hours of sunshine a day even in December. Right into November, daytime temperatures often nudge 70° F. And, while the islands boast few sandy beaches, there are compensations. Summertime brings a round of colorful village festivals complete with fireworks. Diving and sailing are excellent. You can play golf, go horseback riding, attend trotting races. There are theaters, cinemas, and opera.

House prices? Well, A spacious seafront apartment could be yours for $76,500...or you can rent for $4,590 annually. Of course, apartments aren't the only option. Hidden behind high walls are "Houses of Character:" centuries-old dwellings with patios embellished with Arabic-style fountains or citrus trees. Like the islands' smaller farmhouses, these start at just $127,500 for foreign buyers.

Malta is hot—and we don't just mean its summer weather. With little room for new building, values have nowhere to go but up. Prices are likely to rocket further now that Malta has joined the EU. Over the past 20 years, property values have risen by an average 200%. Predictions are for another 100% gain over the next 10 years.

Provided they're in prime locations, upscale apartment residences, seafront properties, spacious villas, farmhouses, and "Houses of Character" are likely to rattle up the highest increases. These are always in demand with foreign buyers.

Malta or Gozo?

Only a mile of sea separates Malta from Gozo but they're distinctively different. Each appeals to a different type of buyer. If you enjoy being surrounded by thousands of people, choose Malta—this bursting-at-the-seams island is effectively a city-state.

Winston Churchill called Malta a "tiny rock of history and romance," but since the war years construction has been relentless...and often a shock to first-time visitors. Radiating from the commercial and business center of Sliema is a huge hodgepodge of modern urban sprawl. Views across Valletta's Grand Harbor towards the Three Cities (the settlements of Vittoriosa, Kalkera, and Senglea) show how Malta's medieval builders also packed them in. For a more village-like ambience, look to the island's south coast, the northwestern tip, and inland around the "Silent City" of Mdina.

With only 95 square miles of territory, Malta is only around the size of Manhattan...yet almost 370,000 people live here. Although some verdant spaces remain—the tiny fields encased in stone walls are reminiscent of what western Ireland would be like under sunny skies —"the Big Island" has one of earth's greatest population densities. It's often hard judging where one town ends and the next begins.

Home to just under 30,000 inhabitants, a minuscule 26 square miles in size, tranquil Gozo provides a nostalgic escape. This is a world of deep blue sea and hidden coves...green fields, prickly pear hedges, and scattered windmills...church spires and sleepy villages. Some farmers still travel by horse and cart, single sheep ride in solitary splendor in toy-sized trucks, and almost all the older generation attend daily mass.

Homes are cheaper than on most parts of Malta, but word is getting out about slow-paced Gozo. Sought-after properties with foreign buyers are its flat-roofed, honey-hued stone farmhouses. They still often surface for around the $125,000 mark.

Maybe you already know the lifestyle you prefer, but do explore both islands. And even if you decide to buy solely for investment purposes, you're unlikely to lose money. Rental returns average an annual 5% to 6.5%, with annual capital appreciation coming in at around 10%.

Apartment living

The least-expensive properties are apartments. Although many are listed as holiday flats, they usually have two or three bedrooms. The average apartment (1,200 square feet is typical) would be large enough for most resident couples.

Malta's most affordable seaside apartments are in the resorts of Bugibba, Qawra, and St. Paul's Bay—there's no problem finding two-bedroom homes for under $90,000 here. Currently on the market in Bugibba, for $84,000, a furnished third-floor apartment with two double bedrooms, combined living-kitchen-dining room, a good-sized balcony, and brand new bathroom. The property includes two air conditioning units, all appliances, and use of roof.

Unfortunately Bugibba and its satellite resorts aren't particularly attractive. Packed with British-style pubs and cafés, they draw budget-minded tourists on cheap package deals.

However, good deals exist elsewhere. In Malta's southeast, $93,000 is sought for a three-bedroom apartment at Marsascala—being sold fully furnished. Here's another listing from the Malta Times. "First-floor seafront apartment in a block of only two with views of St. George's Bay. Accommodation comprises fitted rustic kitchen, living room, two bedrooms, bathroom, and balcony overlooking the bay. Price: $81,600.

Not all apartments are so modestly priced. Senglea is one of the crowded "Three Cities" rising above the Grand Harbor. Alternatively dubbed the Cottonera, the Knights of Malta were based here before they built the golden-stone capital, Valletta. It's medieval, shabby in places, but undeniably atmospheric. A two-bedroom seafront apartment on Senglea promenade is $191,000. Part of a four-unit development, it's finished to a high standard with parquet floors and wrought-iron balconies. It would be lovely to sit on its front balcony at sunset, drinking in views of the Cottonera, Valletta's St. Barbara Bastions, and the new yacht marina.

On Gozo, how about this two-bedroom apartment at Zebbug? Although this village is a little ways inland, nowhere here is far from the sea. Priced at $99,500, its balcony overlooks a green valley and the north coast. Calypso's Cave—where the Greek nymph seduced Ulysses—is within walking distance. So are a couple of small coves.

And the views won't disappear. Planning laws on Gozo bar any new construction outside a village's boundaries. Furthermore, no apartment residence can be higher than three stories in an inland village, and four stories on the coast.

Maisonettes and terraces

Many locals live in maisonettes and terraced houses. A maisonette is a two-storey dwelling with one family above and another below. Prices run the gamut from $115,000 to $480,000. For example, $129,000 is the price of a three-bedroom maisonette at M'scala with a front patio, yard, and sea and country views.

Naxxar is a village in central Malta. Many of its streets are lined with golden-stone maisonettes and terraced houses with pocket hanky-sized gardens. No sea views, but purple bougainvillea cascades over walls, and streets are neat and tidy. A first-floor with three bedrooms in a maisonette lists at $150,500.

In Swieqi, one of Malta's most traditional villages, a first-floor maisonette with three bedrooms, back verandah, roof garden, and garage is $216,000. Prices are even higher around St. Julian's on the coast. Here a two-bedroom maisonette with large private garden, terrace, and views of the bay is $234,000.

At the top of the range, $476,000 is sought for a luxury maisonette with private roof, landscaped gardens, and communal swimming pool in an upmarket at Kappara.

"Houses of Character"

Like farmhouses, these traditional properties often have architectural features such as arched doorways, mill rooms, and inner courtyards. In older properties you may even come across a birthing chamber —generations of pregnant women gave birth in these little rooms in the days before hospital care. Some Houses of Character are 100 years old, others go back to the 17th century. Generally hidden behind high stone walls, most houses look very plain from the outside, but this is deliberate—islanders like their privacy.

Amazingly, prices start at around $75,000. You could still buy an unconverted House of Character in the inland Maltese town of Rabat for this price, with three bedrooms, sitting room, kitchen, dining room, and courtyard. However, under Maltese laws, a foreign buyer would need to spend $52,000 on restoration costs in order to buy this property.

Traditional houses that have been renovated start at $100,000 but a foreign buyer's entry point is $127,500. Location and architectural features attract a premium. A 300-year-old townhouse with three bedrooms, pool, and garage in St. Julians on Malta is $357,000.

Known as the "Silent City," Mdina is an exquisitely preserved citadel town. Stand on its walls, and you look down on a panorama that seems straight from the lands of the Bible. Ribboning out over tiny green fields towards the cobalt blue sea is an almost continuous swathe of flat-roofed white, golden, and biscuit-colored houses. This was Malta's capital during the days of Arab rule in the 9th century. Later, it became a favorite with the palace-building aristocracy. It's tiny though—there are only 1,100 or so residents living behind its golden ramparts.

Homes in Mdina rarely come on the market...and when they do they command hefty prices. Take this converted House of Character with a roof terrace for $209,000. It's described as "ideal for a couple or single person," but it's 880 square feet at most.

Victoria, the tiny island capital of Gozo, is also dominated by a huge citadel, built in the 15th century to provide the islanders with a refuge against pirate raids. For centuries, Gozo's natural harbors were a magnet to sea raiders who prowled inland in search of food, water...and islanders to sell into slavery. Across from Victoria's citadel is St. George's parish, full of quaint meandering alleyways. Many houses here bear wall plaques of St. George slaying the dragon. You can find renovated Houses of Character here from $135,000 to $165,000.

Farmhouses

The word "farmhouse" generally conjures up visions of solitary dwellings set in pastureland. Don't expect to see these types of farmhouses on the Maltese islands. Here they huddle together on village streets. Gozitans kept livestock in their stone farmhouses right up to the 1950s. Farming families lived above the mill room, where beasts were herded at night.

Cows...sheep...goats..poultry? Not any more. Most mill rooms have been converted into spacious lounges—though many owners have kept the old mangers and drinking troughs as architectural features. Like Houses of Character, these types of homes feature Arabic-style archways and inner courtyards. Some have swimming pools...which will appeal to vacation renters. During high summer, a farmhouse sleeping four to six with pool easily rents for $160 a day.

You'll find farmhouses on Malta, but they're in short supply and very expensive. I was shown one with nine rooms and pool at Zebbug—asking price $841,000. A three-bedroom farmhouse with central courtyard and garden with pool in Siggiewi village is currently on the market for $586,000. That's matching Tuscan price levels.

Gozo is a better bet for farmhouses. Although prices have risen 20% to 25% in the last two years, small converted farmhouses (without pool) still pop up for $150,000. Larger ones with pools generally fetch $200,000 to $450,000. Much depends on number of rooms, standard of refurbishment, and the all-important view.

At Xaghra, with lovely sea and country views, a farmhouse is to be sold for $158,000 after it's converted and finished that would make an ideal holiday home. It is to include an open-plan living room/dining room and kitchen, three bedrooms, bathroom, and a shower.

Il Mithna ("The Mill') at Gharb is $166,000. No pool but the central courtyard is charming...and the original external stairs lead to a sun terrace. It's two, double-sized bedrooms are both en-suite. On the outskirts of the village, a converted farmhouse with mill room, combined living/dining area leading onto a courtyard, kitchen, and four double bedrooms plus terrace is $227,000. Down the road, a beautifully restored three-bedroom farmhouse with courtyard, large pool, and deck area is $357,000.

Pronounced "arb," Gharb is old Arabic for the far west. Naturally enough, this village lies on Gozo's western edge. A tangle of rural lanes delivers you to the Azure Window, a natural archway of white stone framing the sapphire sea. Along the coast, Fungus Rock rises from the waters. It's name stems from a type of fungus...and the Knights of Malta discovered that it had healing qualities. It was so highly prized that anyone caught stealing this natural medicine was either condemned to death or sent to the galleys.

Here too is Dwejra's Inland Sea, a noted diving spot. Behind towering cliffs, this huge natural pond is linked to the sea by a tunnel—fishing boats take summer visitors through it to see the Azure Window and Fungus Rock.

Villas

With Malta so short of space, large, modern detached villas or bungalows of 1,500 to 2,000 square feet with pools and sizeable gardens fetch high prices. It's rare to find such villas for under $500,000...though you might get lucky. For $472,000, Perry's has a lovely four-bedroom villa with pool, garage, and outdoor kitchenette at Marsaxlokk in southeast Malta. It has good views of Marsaxlokk Bay, where the Turkish fleet moored during the Great Siege of 1565. Especially as it's being sold furnished, this villa seems to be reasonably priced; you can easily pay more than that.

You can especially pay more around St. Andrews and Madliena's elevated heights in northern Malta. It's prime villa territory and these areas are popular with wealthy Maltese. There are views of unspoiled countryside as well as the sea...and residents awake to the sound of birdsong. Surrounded by a sizeable garden, a luxury villa with pool, deck, BBQ, and separate guest apartment at St. Andrews is listed at $1.09 million. At Madliena, a three-bedroom, two-bathroom semi-detached villa with pool is $762,000.

Specially-designated developments

Developments in specially designated areas (SDAs) are at the market's top end. Non-EU buyers can generally only purchase one home on the Maltese islands—either a house or an apartment. However, in SDAs, you can buy as many homes as you wish.

One of Malta's first SDAs was the exclusive Portomaso waterfront development at St. Julian's. Garnering an array of international awards, this has set the standard for other developments. Now fully completed, over 75% of apartments have been sold. About 35% are Maltese-owned; the British and the Dutch are major foreign buyers. Prices at Portomaso now range from $211,000 for 860-square-foot studios with sea views to $708,000 for spacious 2,800-square-foot penthouse apartments. But get this: those who bought sea-view apartments off-plan have now almost doubled their money.

Framed on three sides by the Mediterranean, Tigné Point development takes its name from the rocky promontory guarding the entrance to the natural harbor of Marsamxett. Halfway between modern Sliema and the twilight splendor of ancient Valletta, the complex was inspired by Malta's town squares. Along with shops, cafés, restaurants, and bars, there are health and leisure facilities, a clubhouse, and shoreline swimming pool. Apartment prices start at $264,000 and rise depending on size, location, and views.

With spectacular views of Valletta and the sea, one of the best apartments is split-level. It has living space of 3,000 square feet, front and side terraces of 504 square feet, and garage. Price is $892,500.

The developers believe the Tigné Point project represents a prime investment and they appear to be right. Most apartments in the first phase (Tigné South) have been purchased off-plan. The first batch of luxury apartments will be completed in 2005 with more units to follow in further stages.

Vittoriosa is one of the Three Cities that rise in a medieval jumble across the Grand Harbor from Valletta. Apartments in the brand-new Cottonera Waterfront Project, designated an SDA, start at $247,000 for a 1,300-square-foot unit. This should be an attractive area, as plans include a new 150-berth yacht marina, outdoor bars, and restaurants.

Rental options

Provided annual rent amounts to at least Lm 1,800 a year or Lm 150 a month ($4,590 a year and $382 monthly), foreigners can live on Malta without buying property—and still take advantage of a 15% income tax rate. Real estate agents such as Frank Salt, Perry, and Legend handle rentals, and Sara Grech's agency has a special office dealing solely with rental property. These furnished homes were available through Frank Salt at the time of writing:

- First-floor apartment at Nadur on the island of Gozo with views across the Gozo channel from the terrace. Accommodation comprises three bedrooms, one bathroom, combined kitchen-dining room, and living area. Monthly rent: $380.

• One-, two- and three-bedroom apartments and penthouses with elevator and use of two freshwater swimming pools. Located in Kappara, an upmarket residential area close to Malta University. Monthly rent: $255 to $510 monthly.

• Two-bedroom, two-bathroom House of Character at Siggiewi with spacious mill room, study, kitchen, eating and living area with fireplace, small garden, and large courtyard. Monthly rent: $765 monthly.

• Two-bedroom House of Character at Senglea, one of Malta's oldest cities. All rooms have sea and harbor views. There's a large terrace for sunbathing or entertaining. Monthly rent: $1,020 monthly.

• On the Sliema sea front (where the locals come out for a *passegiata* or stroll along the promenade in the evenings), a three-bedroom, two-bathroom with wide front balcony and car space. Monthly rent: $1,275 monthly.

• Three-bedroom apartment with balconies all around in old Valletta. Magnificent Grand Harbor sea views and across to the three Cities. Monthly rent: $1,530 monthly.

Incidentally, honey-hued Valletta is one of the Mediterranean's loveliest capitals, built by Malta's most renowned colonizers, the Hospitaller Knights of St. John of Jerusalem. Better known in history books as the Knights of Malta, they fought off the marauding Turks of the Byzantine Empire for over 250 years. Rising above the Grand Harbor, Valletta is an impregnable fortress city that has barely changed since the Knights built it. Stepped streets...dim alleyways...golden palaces...balconied houses with emerald green and sapphire blue shutters. You'll love it.

Malta and Gozo real estate agents

• **Frank Salt Real Estate,** *2 Paceville Avenue, St. Julians, STJ06*

Malta; tel. (356)21-353-696; e-mail: jlupi@franksalt.com.mt; website www.franksalt.com.mt.

- **Perry Estate Agents Ltd.**, *197 Tower Rd, Sliema SLM09 Malta; tel. (356)21-310-800; e-mail: perry@perry.com.mt; website: www. perry.com.mt.*

- **Cassar & Cooper Real Estate**, *St. Anne Court, Tigné Seafront, Sliema, Malta; tel. (356)21-343-730 or (356)21-343-735; e-mail: m.demaria@cassar-cooper.com; website www.realestate.cassar-cooper.com.*

- **Sara Grech Real Estate**, *148 Tower Rd, Sliema SLM 11 Malta; tel. (356)21-342-090 or (356)21-342-092; e-mail: administration@ saragrech.com; website www.saragrech.com.*

- **Frank Salt Real Estate**, *13 Fortunato Mizzi St, Victoria, Gozo; tel. (356)21-560-169; e-mail: gozo@franksalt.com.mt.*

- **Legend Real Estate**, *31 Republic St, Victoria, VCT 103 Gozo; tel. (356)21-558-855; e-mail: gozo@legend.com.mt; website www.legend. com.mt.*

Restrictions

At Xlendi, a Gozo seaside village, a furnished two-bedroom apartment overlooking the bay is listed at $49,700. But you cannot buy it. And you can't buy this quaint converted one-bedroom townhouse in Senglea, with a lovely terrace giving harbor views, listed at $69,000. This is because a minimum purchase price applies to non-Maltese buyers. For apartments, the minimum is $76,500. For houses, it's $127,500.

Although Malta is now a part of the EU, its property laws remain more restrictive than in other member countries. That's because some Maltese people opposed joining the EU as they feared that property values would rise sharply and price locals out of the market. During EU negotiations, the Maltese government held out to keep a minimum price level for foreigners and to restrict them from owning only one property, unless it's in a specially designated area. (In SDAs, you can buy as much real estate as you wish. However, these properties are generally very luxurious and high-priced.)

In view of Malta's size and population density, the EU agreed to most of the demands. However, EU citizens face fewer restrictions than foreign citizens of other countries:

- If an EU citizen has lived on the islands for a continuous period of at least five years, restrictions on purchasing property will be removed. That person will be treated like a local and may buy as many properties at whatever price level that he or she wants. Note, though, that this change only applies to EU citizens—not to North Americans or any other nationality.

- If a foreign citizen wishes to settle in Malta permanently and buy a house, prior authorization is required. No authorization is required for EU citizens. However, as a North American, you must obtain it.

- No authorization will be required for an EU citizen who is a permanent resident to purchase property connected with business activities.

There were restrictions on foreigners letting property, though these have recently been eased. As things stand, you can rent out properties with swimming pools, homes classified by the local tourist authority as "First Class," and SDA properties.

While the minimum purchase price of $127,500 applies to foreign buyers seeking houses, this figure can include any restoration costs. For example, $121,000 buys a House of Character at Zurrieq, a village near Malta's southern coast. "Semi-converted," it comprises hall, kitchen/breakfast room, living room, small dining room, one double bedroom (en-suite), two single bedrooms (one en-suite), and courtyard. Another $20,000 would be needed for full restoration.

Buying your home

Once you've found your Maltese home, you pay a 10% deposit.

Around three months later, the balance is payable upon completion of the exchange of contracts. During this time, the public notary undertakes searches to prove good title. Contracts are written in English. The only additional amounts to pay, over and above the cost of the property, are:

- Stamp duty and transfer levy—5%
- Notarial fees—1%
- Ministry of Finance Permit—$240

Obtaining finance

Depending on income and personal circumstances, you can borrow up to 80% of the property purchase price, if the home loan is designated in Maltese lire—and up to 60% if it is in a major foreign currency. The loan can be repaid over a maximum of 30 years provided an applicant's age does not exceed 65 years upon the last repayment. Through Bank of Valletta, interest rates start at 4.75% per annum.

- **Bank of Valletta,** *Mortgages & Investments (Ethelbert Perini), 3/4 St. John Square, Valletta VLT 10, Malta; tel. (356)21-333-927* or *(356)21-245-252; e-mail: ethelbert.perini@bov.com.*

Residency permits and taxation

You don't have to be a permanent resident to purchase property on the Maltese Islands, though some restrictions do apply.

Non-residents

Providing each stay does not exceed three months, no permits govern non-residents and they are not subject to local tax conditions. However, property purchased must exceed 30,000 Maltese lire for an apartment and 50,000 Maltese lire for a house. As stated earlier, the price may include restoration costs.

Temporary residents

Provided you can show the means to support yourself, you can obtain an extended tourist permit. This allows you to stay on the Maltese Islands for longer than three months and is renewable every six months or annually. Temporary residents are only subject to local income tax if their stay exceeds an aggregate of 182 days in one calendar year.

Tax is payable only on remittances to Malta emanating from income—not capital. Many "temporary" couples bring in an annual amount of around 4,500 Maltese lire ($11,500). The first $11,000 is tax free, and they're charged 15% on the remainder. If more money is needed, they charge items to their home bank credit cards and thus avoid paying Maltese tax.

Maltese tax rates for temporary residents

Married Couples		Single Person	
First Lm 4,300	tax free	First Lm 3,100	tax free
Next Lm 1,700	15%	Next Lm 1,000	15%
Next Lm 1,250	20%	Next Lm 900	20%
Next Lm 1,250	25%	Next Lm 1,000	25%
Next Lm 1,500	30%	Next Lm 750	30%
Over Lm 10,000	35%	Over Lm 6,750	35%

Permanent residents

Only permanent foreign residents can obtain the 15% flat rate of income tax. To qualify, you must have an annual income of 10,000 Maltese lire ($25,500) or proven capital of 150,000 Maltese lire ($382,500). This capital doesn't have to be remitted to Malta, apart from the amount needed to purchase a home. However, changes in the Maltese budget for 2003 upped the minimum annual income to be brought into the country from 6,000 Maltese lire (plus 1,000 Maltese lire for each dependent) to 12,000 Maltese lire ($30,600). Irrespective of the number of dependents, the minimum tax payable by a permanent resident has now increased to 1,800 Maltese lire ($4,590).

If you own a property, you are allowed to rent it out. Rental income is subject to the prevailing rate of income tax.

There are no inheritance taxes in Malta. However, on the death of a permanent resident who owns property, there are stamp duties calculated at a flat rate of 5% on the value of a home.

Cost of living

A Maltese bank clerk supports a family on an annual salary of around $13,000. That's a good indication of how affordable living here can be. There are no property taxes or local authority rates to pay.

Monthly water and electricity bills are approximately $70 for apartments, and about $150 for farmhouses or villas with pools. Bottled gas, used for cooking, costs around $7 per canister. However, foreigners aren't always as cost-efficient as locals. They tend to spend a lot more than locals on utilities. If you leave lights on, taps running, and indulge in other wasteful habits, you could be spending as much as $350 a month on water and electricity.

Regarding shopping and eating out, the average British couple —and most foreign buyers in Malta are British—spends around the equivalent of $825 per month.

Eating out can be cheap or profligate. If you hanker for an English-style breakfast (bacon, egg, and sausage served with tea and toast), you'll find numerous cafés where such a spread only costs $2.50. For $8, you can have a mighty plate of pasta and shellfish in The Stone Crab, a waterfront restaurant in Xlendi, a Gozitan seaside village.

The locals have an odd fondness for stewed rabbit. If you acquire the taste, a plate of rabbit casserole served with fries, salad, and a glass of wine costs around $6.50. Italian-style restaurants abound and seafood is superb.

Cinema tickets are $6.50...a frothy cappuccino $1.25...CDs in Valletta's Sunday market $5.10. Prices of grocery items from a mini-market in Mgarr: four large crusty rolls, 60 cents; one pound of rice, 45 cents; one pound of potatoes, 27 cents; and one pound of apples 33 cents. A liter of Kinnie, a delicious local soft drink made from oranges and herbs, sells for 80 cents.

Health care is excellent. The World Health Organization rates Malta's standard of care as the world's fifth-highest. Doctors make house calls. The charge for a visit from a private doctor is $15 to $25.

When you decide to sell

Non-residents, and temporary and permanent residents are allowed to sell their property at the prevailing market value. The total sale price—including proceeds from movables—may be repatriated anywhere abroad and in any currency.

A capital gains tax of 35% may be charged on the sale of immovable property. This is based on the gains realized after taking into consideration the cost of purchase and sale, as well as any improvements carried out on the property. The tax is not charged on the sale of properties that have been the owner's place of residence for the last three years.

Chapter 6

Portugal

In Europe's southwest corner, sun-kissed Portugal has a rich maritime past, time-warp towns, and an appealing landscape mosaic of hills, rivers, citrus groves, and vineyards. Its population of 10 million enjoys a fairly inexpensive cost of living, though they do pay high sums for homes.

But if you're seeking a land where tradition thrives, Portugal can't be faulted. Singers in dark, poky bars wail melancholic *fado* songs of loss and lament, and hawkers sell sardines from buckets. You can still encounter outdoor barbers in Lisbon's Alfama neighborhood. Houses, churches—even railway stations—are adorned with decorative tiles known as *azulejos*. The Portuguese learned this tile-making technique from the Moors, and *azulejos* are still being made today.

Of course, some areas are more "traditional" than others. Most foreign buyers are drawn to the Algarve, the country's southern coastal fringe. With its Atlantic-swept sandy beaches and top-notch golf courses, this region extends from the Spanish border westwards to Cape St. Vincent.

In the early 1960s, the Algarve had nothing much to offer beside beaches, cliffs, and orange groves. Today, the region derives most of its income comes from tourism. Beaches are still golden and unspoiled, the sea glitters sapphire, and the orange blossoms smell just as sweet—but don't think you'll have the Algarve all to yourself.

There's also a growing appetite for properties near Lisbon, particularly in the coastal resorts of Cascais and Estoril, and in the hills around Sintra.

Stricter planning laws thankfully have ended the haphazard

development of the kind of high-rise blocks that have spoiled much of Spain's southern coast. Today's large-scale developments in coastal Portugal are focused on low-rise, less-imposing buildings grouped around a communal leisure facility.

After some years in the doldrums, the Portuguese property market is on the march again. On the Algarve, prices have risen an average 50% in the last five years. Elsewhere, buy the right property and it's reasonable to anticipate an annual net return from rentals of 8% to 12%. (Plus, of course, capital appreciation.) And although you cannot expect a huge amount from back-street apartments, some golf villas pull in annual rental income of $20,000 and more.

Portugal's Algarve...where life's a beach

Europe's best beaches...3,000 annual sunshine hours...a gorgeous countryside of rich red earth, orange groves, and cork oak forests...excellent infrastructure and amenities...cheap public transport and living costs...delectable seafood for next-to-nothing. You can enjoy plates of clams for under $8.

Such factors make the Algarve the top choice for many European retirees and buyers of second homes. The Algarve's name comes from the Arabic *Al Gharb*—The Western Land. Controlled for 500 years by the Moors, their influence is still visible in the region's architecture. Visit Tavira and you'll see squat, flat-roofed houses with facades covered in shiny plain or patterned tiles. Another Moorish legacy is latticed doors, made of thin interwoven strips of wood. So are the curious white "lace-work' chimneys"...the orange groves...the almond, carob, and olive trees. The Moors considered the Algarve their garden.

Although this is the Atlantic, the shelter of cliffs and coves makes the climate feel Mediterranean-like. Only when you round the region's far western tip do the winds strengthen. Naturally, this brings no complaints from windsurfers.

If you're not in the market for a traditional cottage at the back of beyond, house prices may come as a shock. Most villas cost from $420,000 to over $1 million. Even modest two-bedroom homes in urbanizations away from the beach easily fetch $210,000.

Three British buyers recently entered sealed bids on a villa with an asking price of $817,000 at the Penina golf estate near Lagos. The agents reckon it will achieve over $860,000. For a villa like this, annual running costs are around $20,000—utilities, telephone, local taxes, and maintenance. After deducting 15% agents' commission and 25% income tax, rental income has been around $26,000 over the last six months.

Why are prices so high? Sky-high demand...restrictive building laws...lack of space. The region is only 100 miles long and 35 miles wide.

Is the Algarve built-up? Yes and no. Although developers haven't brutalized the landscape in the same fashion as on Spain's Costa del Sol, five million holiday makers fly into the regional airport at Faro every year. They all have to stay somewhere. Much of the coastline from Faro to Lagos lies under developments. However, only two central Algarve resorts are high-rise horror: Praia da Rocha and Quarteira. Even here, beaches are classic—magnificent golden sands backed by red-gold cliffs.

But go east, west, or a few miles inland, and the "traditional Algarve" still exists. Sardines and lobster pots, sheep and orange groves, gypsy fleamarkets, and convents...all survive intact. With a backdrop of low wooded hills that turn lavender at twilight, the inland Algarve remains world apart...but traditional cottages can be small and primitive. Unfortunately few bargains exist, even here.

Cottages are no longer in abundant supply. Although buying a rural cottage in the Algarve hinterland used to be the cheapest way of getting onto the property ladder, there is now a shortage of traditional countryside properties. Even tumbledown heaps of stones with less than an acre of land often cost over $120,000.

Least expensive at the time of writing is through ERA of Lagos: a two-bedroom village house at Barao San Miguel for $61,000. Poky, however—certainly no room for an American-style kitchen. It also needs much modernization and repair.

For $354,000, Finespo has a charmingly restored Algarvean farmhouse in the hills above Picota. Close to both the market town of Loule and Boliqueime, it comes with valley and coastal views from its terrace. Beaches and golf are about a 20-minute drive away. With three bedrooms, the farmhouse has a number of individual features including bread oven, open fireplace, period frames, beams, thick walls, and large covered area. The 16,000-square-foot walled garden has a variety of fruit trees.

The Western Algarve

Gateway to the western Algarve, Lagos is a genuine town, not simply a beach resort. With a population of 17,500, it's blessed with wonderful beaches on both sides. Apart from the fortified walls, few traces of its early past remain, but its historical baggage goes back to Roman times. The town's old-fashioned core is adorned with tile-faced buildings and Baroque churches glittering with gold leaf. Cobbled streets climb past whitewashed urban cottages; leafy *pracas* (squares) are flanked by antique shops, art galleries and good-value restaurants.

Compared with some other areas of the Algarve, prices are fairly reasonable within Lagos: apartments of 1,000 square feet list for $114,000 to $120,000. A newly constructed corner house in the old quarter is $140,000...but living space is only 660 square feet. A 1,375-square-foot apartment at the new 430-berth marina is $199,000.

A coastal path dips along cliff tops to Ponta da Piedade (Piety Point), where mysterious, small rocks resemble stepping stones to another realm. Called Costa d'Ouro (the Golden Coast) this two-mile section of coastline has golden cliffs wrapped around six sandy coves. The prettiest is Praia Dona Ana, but up above, the developers haven't been inactive.

Coves get crowded in summertime, but Meia Praia has bags of room. (*Praia* means beach.) This three-mile golden sweep is a 25-minutes' walk east of Lagos. There's been a flurry of new development between Lagos Marina and Meia Praia, but it's minimal compared with what arcs east around Lagos Bay. That endless hodgepodge of white in the distance? Alvor...Portimao...Carvoveiro...Praia da Rocha.

Construction activity indicates Meia Praia will be the next "new" resort. Although there are some pretty villas a couple of miles from town, apartment residences nearer Lagos are boxy. Even so, agents are seeking $126,000 to $180,000 for one- and two-bedroom apartments.

Available through Hampton's, the Jardim da Meia Praia development is classier. Set in large landscaped gardens with water features and orangery, it's due for completion in 2004. The complex includes a communal area, tennis court, playground with sandpit, and poolside bar and restaurant. According to the agents, the development offers fantastic rental potential. All apartments have three bedrooms and top-floor apartments have a roof terrace with hot tub and sea view. There are two- and three-bedroom townhouses remaining with a small private garden and option of a Jacuzzi. Prices start at $312,000.

West of Lagos, the coast is fretted with secret coves, ochre-colored rock formations, and pretty fishing settlements. Much of it is inside Costa Vicentina National Park. Planning laws are so strict that it seems unlikely it will ever be encased by concrete. There's some development around Praia da Luz, Burgau, and Salema villages, but it's all low-key.

Although Praia da Luz is a resort, it retains much of the charm of its former identity as a whitewashed fishing village. On the road to Burgau, a two-bedroom duplex apartment with sea view, communal pool, and gardens lists at $146,000. Within the village, a restored blue-and-white fisherman's cottage is $266,000. Three-bedroom villas with pools go from $280,000 for resales to around $390,000 brand-new.

Over the four summer months, the average weekly rental for three-bedroom villas at Praia da Luz is $1,700 gross. After allowing for agency commissions, management, maid service, and income tax, this equates to an average weekly income of $1,000 between June and September.

Sagres is the last village before Europe finally runs out at Cabo San Vicente. The Romans considered it the end of the world, naming it Promontorium Sacrum (Sacred Promontory). Legends abound, including one about St. Vicente, whose martyred remains were supposedly delivered here by a crow.

Blue sea, brightly painted boats, golden rocks, and small sandy beaches...Sagres is lovely, but properties are rare. As with other western Algarve villages, most sell through Lagos agents. ERA has a couple of modest Sagres houses: a 1,400-square-foot home for $149,000 and a slightly larger one for $183,000.

Set in a walled garden of semi-tropical plants and trees, a three-bedroom, three-bathroom villa (2,363 square feet) is $360,000. The property has lounge and dining room, fitted kitchen, pantry/utility room, gym, garage, central heating, and double-glazing. It also a one-bedroom, self-contained apartment with sun terrace above the villa. This is listed at the British property website: *www.escape2portugal.co.uk.*

The Central Algarve

Although the central Algarve won't suit everybody, those with an eye on capital appreciation shouldn't ignore the investment potential. Along with the most amenities and best infrastructure, it has the largest group of foreign residents...and visitors.

Many people prefer cosmopolitan resorts to sleepy towns and villages. If you're thinking of investment—buying something you'll spend little time in—popularity cannot be ignored. A cottage up an unpaved track and miles from anywhere won't rent for fabulous sums...or have many takers.

Vacationers usually have certain requirements. A pool—either private or communal. Easy beach access, and a choice of shops and restaurants. And, on the Algarve, they usually demand a nearby golf course. Two- or three-bedroom homes are most marketable—and also easiest to resell.

Albufeira is the central Algarve's tourism hotspot. It's overbuilt, but since it has few high-rise monstrosities, it's not hideous. With tiers of houses rising above the clifftops and the red-gold beach, the effect is more like an amphitheater. Things heat up during July and August, but on winter weekends it's largely given over to European seniors and Portuguese families exploring the old pedestrianized Moorish quarter.

With 16,000 permanent residents, Albufeira has excellent amenities. Another 24,000 people live in Albufeira *commune* (district) which covers almost 20 miles and includes 23 beaches. Sought-after satellite suburbs include Santa Eulalia, Praia da Ouro, and Olhas da Agua.

Most Albufeira apartments list as having sea views. Sounds good —but the sea can be glimpsed from the bus station—a mile back from the beach. Prices are all over the place, but you can find plenty of studios or one-bedroom apartments from around $72,000, and apartments of 1,320 square feet for under $120,000. Townhouses are $210,000-$420,000, and detached villas fetch $360,000 to $1.8 million.

Praia da Rocha. One local guidebook sums up its essence perfectly. "A resort which is unashamedly a resort...a great beach...bars you will feel instantly at home in." (Note: only if you're a soccer-mad Brit.) "If you have visited the Costa del Sol and enjoyed it you are bound to like Praia da Rocha."

The beach is superb but the resort itself is full of concrete blocks and tourist tat. Downmarket...overpriced...but roast beef and Yorkshire pud are an undoubted selling point for some British buyers. Apartments of 660 square feet start at around $126,000, and 880-square-foot apartments in residences with pools fetch $162,000.

Praia da Rocha was first developed in the 1960s and it shows. There are only three small slots in which to glimpse the sea from the promenade. It's like walking through a tunnel. On the plus side, it's only a 10-minute drive from the real shops and restaurants in Portimao, a working town whose 36,000 residents are almost all Portuguese. Prices there are more sensible—a 1,350-square-foot central zone apartment is $98,000. But you may not be taken with its nondescript high-rises.

Alvor is the nicest resort hereabouts. Development is mostly low-rise...there's a small quarter of whitewashed old houses...a clutch of fish restaurants...plus the Penina estate's three golf courses on the doorstep. Typical for Alvor, a 1,870-square-foot villa is $456,000. Even 770-square-foot apartments fetch $114,000. Agents John R. Evans have a three-bedroom, four-bathroom villa with pool on a small development near Penina golf club. With living space of 2,600 square feet and gardens of 21,500 square feet, this lists for $529,000.

With four golf courses, classy Vilamoura IS the Algarve for many visitors. Yet it's not all about teeing off. The resort town has faultless beaches and a Marina with over 1,000 berths—busy even in winter. Its all-year population is 5,000 to 6,000 and there's a health center, super-markets, and myriad restaurants.

While Vilamoura isn't "traditional," it's no concrete jungle like next-door Quarteira. Most hotels are mega-sized, but the harbor develop-ment, Praia Marina, is a pretty picture of pastel-colored townhouses. There's also Falesia beach, backed by orange-red cliffs.

Quality properties are expensive. For a 1,320-square-foot, semi-detached townhouse near Vilamoura's Pinhal course (a 25-minute walk from the marina), the minimum is $240,000. A 1,400-square-foot apartment overlooking the marina is $300,000. The least expensive vil-las with private pools—1,300 square feet—cost $450,000. Most villas are around the $575,000 mark. At that level you can expect annual net rental income of between $18,000 and $24,000. The above properties are through Vendavilla, an official agent for Vilamoura development.

Cheaper options do exist. One- and two-bedroom apartments list for $132,000 to $173,000—but not on the marina. ERA had a small, one-bedroom semi-detached holiday villa in a closed condominium, with pool and gardens, for $180,000. (Most houses are described as vil-las, even row houses.)

Villas in Quinta da Lago and neighboring Vale da Lobo rarely sur-face for under $1.5 million. And Vale da Lobo's Royal course is top range—it costs $162 to play a round. There are plenty of alternatives, though. The Algarve has 19 golf complexes and 26 individual courses—and they're still creating more. Most charge around $90 for 18 holes but a few offer "twilight" deals from $24 per round.

The Eastern Algarve

East of Faro, seascapes change to lagoons, salt pans, and ribbon-like island spits outlined with long sandy beaches. It's wonderful for birdwatchers and you'll also see locals digging for crabs, cockles, and razor clams. In single-street fishing villages, men mend nets, chickens wander cobbled lanes—the traditional Algarve lifestyle prevails.

With only one brash touristy resort—Monte Gordo—foreign buyers haven't yet ventured east in numbers. Quiet fishing villages include Cabanas, Fuzeta, and Luz de Tavira. Still, villas with pools and sea views easily fetch $270,000, and more. Tavira agents IMO 90 have a lovely Fuzeta property: a two-storey 1,500-square-foot villa with balconies, covered terraces, swimming pool, and large garden. Price: $533,000.

Tavira is a likeable town of 13,000 residents. It snoozes on both banks of the river Gilao, a couple of miles from the lagoon. Palm-lined avenues swell into neat squares, locals sit in *pastelarias* (pastry shops) munching *pasteis de nata* (custard tarts) and filling out lottery tickets. An historic center—all steep-staired alleys—winds past churches and faded Renaissance palaces to a ruined castle. From its battlements, you get incredible views out to the Ria Formosa. During summer, ferryboats cross to the lagoon's islands.

Patricia of Algar Vila agency says it's mostly Swedes and Norwegians buying. However, a dearth of Brits and Germans doesn't mean low prices. The agency is listing "a beautiful town house" for $188,000. Disappointingly, the 1,100-square-foot urban cottage doesn't much resemble the photo. Although restored inside, outside plasterwork was shabby...and the house next door was derelict. You could negotiate—it's acceptable to offer 3% to 10% less than the asking price—but it's understandable why most buyers want modern homes. Some of Tavira's "shabby chic" traditional properties have been on the market for years, not months.

Attached townhouses under construction in Tavira's urbanizations start at $134,000, but they're only around 880 square feet. Even 385-square-foot studios fetch $72,000. A 1,150-square-foot split-level house within walking distance of town is $210,000. One good buy is through IMO 90—a 1,850-square-foot villa built in 1994. It's two miles from Tavira but only a few minutes' walk from a lagoon. Price: $239,000.

Foraging inland, Algar is asking $208,000 for a restored windmill nine miles from Tavira. With land of 32,000 square feet, it has a double bedroom on the ground floor that is separated from the kitchen by a covered veranda. There's a fireplace, bathroom, alcove for a sofabed, and 360-degree views over hills to the sea. Water is from a borehole.

Vila Real de San Antonio is the last stop before the Spanish border. (You can take a passenger ferry across the Guadiana River to Ayamonte in Spain for $1.25). A neat frontier town of arrow-straight streets and squares bedecked with orange trees, Vila Real de San Antonio only dates back to 1774. It was built in just five months...an earlier settlement was destroyed by a tidal wave.

A renovated townhouse of 880 square feet is $164,000 through ERA's local office. For the best-value properties, follow the Guadiana River into the countryside. In Alcoutim, an inland border town, a restored rustic house of 1,100 square feet is $120,000.

Algarve realtor contacts

- **ERA** (Jan Dirk Hofman), *rua 25 de Abril, no 46, 8601-904 Lagos; tel. (351)282-769342; e-mail: lagos@era.pt; website: www.era.pt.*

- **Garveighs** (Armenio Cintra), *Av dos Descobrimentos 43F, 8600-645 Lagos; tel. (351)282-769-341; e-mail: armeniocintra@garveigh.com; website: www.garveigh.com.*

- **Hamptons International—Portugal,** *Avenida das Comunidades Portuguesas, Edificio Lapinha, A & R/C, 8600-501 Lagos; tel. (351)282-789-336; website www.hamptons-portugal.com.*

- **Finespo,** *Rua Joacquim Martins Rodrigues 107, 8200-448 Guia-Albufeira; tel. (351)289 –560-261; e-mail: tim@finespo-algarve.com; website: www.finespo-algarve.com.*

- **John R. Evans** (Filipa Silva), *Rua Judice Biker 35, PT-8500-701 Portimao; tel. (351)282-411-206; e-mail: realsol@ip.pt; website: www.johnevansrealsol.com.*

- **Vendavila** (Lora Café), *Marina Plaza, Loja 69, Av da Marina, Vilamoura; tel. (351)289-389-646; e-mail: vilagente@mail.telepac.pt;*

website: www.vendavila.com.

- **Algar Vila** (Patricia Alexandre), *Travessa das Cunhas 29, 8800-372 Tavira; tel. (351)281-324-115; e-mail: rdd71069@mail.telepac.pt; website: www.algarvila.com.*

- **IMO 90** (Sandra Silvestre), *rua 1 de Maio 30A, 8800-360 Tavira; tel. (351)281-324-684.*

The lure of Lisbon

On the roll call of western European capitals, Lisbon probably has the lowest profile of all. But it's gorgeous. Come evening, the sunset sets everything aglow: pale pink palaces turn to deep tangerine...waterfront palm trees turn to emerald...the Tagus estuary and the Atlantic beyond glitter silvery blue...the battlements above Sao Jorge's Castle look saintly with its golden halo.

The castle looms above the Alfama, Lisbon's labyrinthine old Moorish quarter of dim alleys, archways, and paint-peeled buildings, which itself rises above the Tagus Estuary like a ramshackle house of cards. It escaped the 1775 earthquake and the atmosphere is gratifyingly medieval. Balconies are laden with flapping laundry and pots of geraniums, canaries trill cadenzas inside tiny cages, men sit playing cards. Flights of crumbling stone stairways clamber ever upwards—in some parts it's just too steep for streets.

Property bargains in Lisbon are few, but this would be a great city to rent a home for a while—a furnished one-bedroom apartment in a good neighborhood is available right now for $660 monthly. The climate is kind, and if you ever tire of Lisbon's curiosities, miles of Atlantic beaches are almost on the doorstep.

Including the metropolitan area, Lisbon's population is almost 2.5 million. Although very much a modern city, you have to ride the metro to see the evidence. Tourists rarely stray from the downtown area of 18th century architecture and neighboring medieval quarters. In traditional areas, it's all old world charm...a city made up of separate little villages. However, most residents live in modern suburbs which sprawl out like an octopus's tentacles north of downtown.

Certain neighborhoods are more prestigious—and thus pricier —than others. Some quarters are as shabby as back-street Naples; others are a picture of gracious 18th century formality.

In downtown Lisbon, you can't get any more central than the Rossio, at the bottom of the mile-long Avenida da Liberdade. (On summer Sundays this avenue hosts fleamarkets, outdoor *tai chi* groups, gardening classes, and more.) However, you will pay dearly to live here. A 375-square-foot refurbished studio on the Rossio square is listed with George Knight at $105,000.

Much of the Alfama and Bairro Alto neighborhoods still seem fairly ramshackle, but prices indicate that these areas are up and coming. Cascais agents Rentavila (who also has sales and rental properties in Lisbon and Sintra) is offering a two-bedroom apartment (1,200 square feet) in the Alfama for $280,000.

North of the Alfama, Graca is a *zona tipica*—a traditional neighborhood that has already become quite gentrified. High on a hill, most properties have lookouts over Lisbon's red-tiled rooftops to the Atlantic. Here two-bedroom apartments (1,180 square feet) in new apartment blocks are now fetching almost $300,000.

West of Bairro Alto, it's a 20-minute stroll through switchback streets to Santa Caterina neighborhood. This is another traditional *zona tipica* in the process of getting spruced up. Not quite as scruffy as Bairro Alto, its streets dive down to the waterfront. A refurbished three-bedroom apartment with *vista panoramica* and 1400 square feet of living space lists for $210,000.

Close enough to downtown but without the traffic chaos, is Lapa, one of Lisbon's most sought-after traditional districts. Next-door to Santa Caterina, agents call it a *bairro de prestigio,* a posh neighborhood. The 19th century residences are in excellent repair, there are lots of little shops, and cafés carry window advertisements offering guitar and cello lessons. Diplomats often live in Lapa and it's where Lisbon's middle-class aspires to own homes. A 1,611-square-foot apartment with views down to the Tagus River is currently on the market for $311,000.

Old-style residential areas close by include Campo de Ourique and Estrela. Many buildings date from around 1900. In a refurbished apartment house in Campo de Ourique, a 483-square-foot studio is $108,000. Over in Estrella, a 1400-square-foot apartment is $281,000.

Beyond downtown, the main mass of suburbs has scant visual appeal with the exception of Parque das Nacoes, a desirable enclave that has risen around the 1998 Expo site. Here an 860-square-foot apartment costs $233,000. Six miles east of downtown, packed with new bars and restaurants, Parque das Nacoes feels rather like Barcelona's spanking new waterfront. Full of shiny new apartments, it includes one residence designed like a ship's prow. Every owner has his or her own indoor swimming pool.

Even on winter weekends, lots of local families visit for the day. Attractions include cable cars, a dinky train, a Virtual Reality pavilion, a Live Science Center and the world's second largest Oceanarium. There's a mega-mall—the Vasco da Gama—but the sight that really stops you in your tracks is the Vasco da Gama Bridge stretching for 13 miles over the Tagus.

Elsewhere in the city's modern suburbs, prices for two-bedroom properties start at around $138,000. Much depends on the street, condition of building, proximity to a metro station, etc. Northwest along the metro line, Benfica is a sprawling suburb composed of housing built during the 1960s and 1970s. Square-foot prices are mostly in the $220 to $280 range. It's rather a soulless suburb but the Colombo mall—open until midnight—has more than 400 shops, restaurants, and an entertainment complex.

- **Agencia George Knight,** *Edificio Avis, Av. Fontes Pereira de Melo 35—No. 18 B, 1050-118 Lisboa; tel. (351)21-354-0001; e-mail: gknet@esoterica.pt; website: www.georgeknight.pt.*

- **Lammi Agencia,** *Av. Fontes de Pereira de Melo 31, No. 4 A e B, 1050-117 Lisboa; tel. (351)21-319-3900; e-mail: lisboa@lammi.pt; website: www.lammi.pt.*

- **Libris,** *rua de Sant'Ana a Lapa 67A, 1200-797 Lisboa; tel . (351)21-393-3030; e-mail: libris@libris.pt; website www.libris.pt.*

Spellbinding Sintra

Magnificent, moody Sintra. Inland from Lisbon, a 45-minute train journey from Rossio Station, this town belongs in a gothic novel. A real fairytale place, many of its older houses resemble baronial mansions found in the Scottish Highlands—all squinting windows, turrets, and miniature battlements. There's even a Scottish flavor to the National Palace. It has two white conical chimneys just like those on Highland whiskey distilleries.

Overlooked by a ruined Moorish castle, Sintra once served as a summer capital for Portugal's royal family. Its misty hills still provide a retreat for wealthy Lisboites. Full of palaces, gargoyles, and mossy grottos, the town's romantic aura has inspired artists, writers, and poets for centuries. "Glorious Eden," expounded Lord Byron, who said it was filled with "beauties of every description, natural and artificial. Palaces and gardens rising in the midst of rocks, cataracts and precipices; convents on stupendous heights, a distant view of the sea and the Tagus."

Charming chapels, buildings with tiled facades, sunny cafés, dappled-shadow gardens, fan-tailed white pigeons fluttering from wooden dovecotes, mysterious-looking Moorish gateways leading to turreted houses poking out of the trees...Byron's Sintra is still recognizable. In fact, it's a World Heritage Site. If you want to explore in the old-fashioned way, horse-drawn carriages clip-clop around town.

But 17th or 18th century townhouses in old Sintra rarely come to market. Those that do are priced accordingly—you're unlikely to get change from $700,000 for any period property here. Things are more affordable in Sintra's new part. Lammi has a 540-square-foot apartment for $98,000; in the Algueirao-Mem Martins neighborhood, a 750-square-foot apartment is $101,500. A modern house (3,000 square feet including terrace) with garden and views of the Sintra hills is $404,000.

Old houses to restore in nearby villages start at around $100,000, with refurbishment costs coming in at an additional $50,000 to $60,000.

- **Lammi Sintra,** *Av. dos Bons Amigos No. 38 - 1, 2735-073 Cacém-Sintra; tel. (351)21-913-8100; e-mail: sintra@lammi.pt; website: www.lammi.pt.*

Bargains remain in Estramadura

North of Lisbon's coastal area is Estredamura. It's mainly agricultural, but also fringed by Portugal's best fishing grounds, the source of mussels, lobsters, sea bass, red mullet, and all kinds of piscine delights. One of its prettiest towns is Ericeira (you pronounce it Erishay-eera), a working port of quaint blue-and-white cottages with glorious beaches on its doorstep.

Old Ericeira was founded in the 13th century. "The Fishermen's Quarter" is a place of cobbled lanes, tiny *marisqueira* seafood restaurants and bleached white cottages, many carrying little plaques of azulejo tiles honoring different saints. It's lovely...not every little house is trimmed with vivid blue paintwork, but so many are that it's just like wandering around a fishing community in the Greek Cyclades.

Village houses in reasonable condition from 1,075 to 1,300 square feet still often sell for under $120,000 in Estremadura. And compared to the Cascais-Estoril, that is reasonable. Old cottages—habitable but needing some renovation work—can be had for $80,000, sometimes less. Restoration projects surface for around $50,000.

On listings, a traditional village house is usually called a *casa de aldeia* or a *moradia de aldeia.* You'll also see *casas rusticas* (rural houses). These aren't necessarily old—they can be brand-new, and many are. They're not ugly...strict planning rules are now enforced.

Currently available through Ericeira Real Estate for $113,700 is a bleached-white village house at Pucerica, three miles from Ericeira and the beaches. Living space is 1,265 square feet. The house has a small patio, two bedrooms, living room with kitchenette, bathroom, storage room, and a wine cellar that still needs some work. For $128,700, you could buy a more modern 2,100-square-foot house that's five miles from Ericeira and only a couple of miles from Assetta Beach.

Within Ericeira, a top-floor studio with balcony is $95,800. New two-bedroom apartments list from $132,000 to $147,000, with two-bedroom terraced townhouses fetching $180,000.

- **Ericeira Real Estate** (Aida Grades or Luisa Marques), *Praca de Republica 2, Loja-13, 2655-249 Ericeira; tel. (351)261-862-633; e-mail: vendas@ericeira-imob.com; website: www.ericeira-imob.com.*

The Costa do Estoril

The Costa do Estoril is the name given to the coastline stretching southwest of the capital. While there are some lovely homes here, North Americans are unlikely to think they're great value. Thing is, resorts such as Estoril and Cascais are within 35 minutes of Lisbon. That's commuting distance...and local buyers pay high sums for the privilege of such a location.

Although summers here aren't as hot as the Algarve, it's still warm —on average, 82° F. In deepest winter it gets down to the mid-50s Fahrenheit, but many days bring clear blue skies and sunshine. You can still sit outside at lunchtimes, feasting on plump grilled sardines or *pasteis de bacalhau* (cod fishcakes) served with delicious potatoes and salad for under $8, wine included.

Near Lisbon, the coastline is overdeveloped. It's not appealing—in fact some resort towns suggest the architectural blueprint came courtesy of the old Soviet bloc. With its forest of high-rises trimmed a sickly yellow, Sao Pedro looks particularly ghastly. Stay on the train...

Things improve at Estoril, but sadly the 1960s planners couldn't leave well alone. The elegant villas that gave Estoril aristocratic cachet are now flanked by some unsightly concrete developments. If royalty still vacation here, they're probably third-rank hangers-on. While it undoubtedly attracts an upmarket class of tourism, you may feel it has an almost jaded air.

There is no point in even looking for small apartments in quality residences for less than $100,000. For something more spacious, around 970 square feet, you'll pay in the region of $180,000.

However, there are some super beaches and six golf courses in the Estoril area—and it's also on Grand Prix auto-racing circuit. The Estoril casino describes itself as Europe's largest. If super-jackpot payouts of $800,000 make your eyes gleam, it may be your kind of haunt.

Cascais (pronounced Cash-ky-eesh) is a 30-minute stroll on foot from Estoril. Part sophisticated town, part sunshine resort, it's very agreeable with black-and-white mosaic pavements, street signs made of *azulejos*, and a sparkling new marina. There's also a genuine fish market among the lobster pots down on the quay. The town has three small coves flanked by rock formations—among them rose-gold Praia da Rainha (Queen's Beach).

Like in Estoril though, prices are a bit silly. As Aida Grades in Ericeira later explained when we spoke about price disparity, "It's like buying a coat. Some are more expensive than others, but it's still a coat. In Cascais you're paying for a designer label."

For a "very cozy" whitewashed house at Areia-Cascais near the beach, you'll pay a designer price of $258,000 for your extremely tight 540 square feet of living space. Something more spacious? A five-bedroom bungalow-style villa in the Quinta da Beloura development is $552,000.

Apartments in Cascais don't seem to follow any kind of square-foot science. Depending on location, you can spend $180,000 and get anything from 485 square feet to 1,020 square feet of living space. One of the least expensive apartments on the market costs $99,000, but it's only 515 square feet. A price of $300,000 is sought for a 1,880-square-foot duplex in a luxury development at Bicuda, just outside Cascais. Barrio do Rosario is one of the most sought-after Cascais neighborhoods—here an 860-square-foot apartment is $176,000.

North of Cascais, you have the pounding Atlantic on one side, and the low hills of the *Serra de Sintra* on the other. Unlike the stretch of coast between Lisbon and Estoril, this area is completely unspoiled, probably due to the steep cliffs. Villages such as Biscaia, Azoia, and Ulgeira aren't beachfront, but their high position means incredible vistas of ocean and green hills densely clad with trees. It's quiet, traditional, and very beautiful. Stone walls are smothered in cascades of purple morning-glories.

In the surrounding countryside, villas, farmhouses, and *casas rusticas* (rural houses) fetch astounding sums—and they usually sell as soon as they hit the market. Through Rentavila, a country-style house with garden and swimming pool at Malveira da Serra is $474,000. For substantial farmhouses in good condition, you're nudging into million-dollar territory. As for villas—$780,000 is the asking price of a villa with 1800 square feet of living space.

- **Rentavila,** *Rua Marques Leal Pancada, 24 2750-430 Cascais; tel. (351)21-482-7075; e-mail: rentavila@rentavila.com; website: www. rentavila.com.*

- **Sofia Cabral,** *Farmhouse Properties, rua Frederico Arouca, 43-2 Piso, 2750 Cascais; tel. (351)21-484-8163, (351)21-484-8164 or (351)21-484-8166; fax (351)21-483-6426; e-mail: farmhouse@ mail.telepac.pt.*

- **ERA Parede,** *Av. Dos Maristas 518, 2775-242 Parede; tel. (351)21-484-7300; fax: (351)214-531-443; e-mail: parede@era.pt; website: www.era.pt.*

Buy-to-let

Buying off-plan is common on the Algarve, though buy-to-let deals like those in France are still in their infancy. But you can find some on the Algarve. The main attraction of buy-to-let here is the high rental yields. It's not just a summer season on the Algarve—during the winter, golfers are seeking apartments and villas as close to the courses as they can.

Near Lagos in the western Algarve, a new luxury golf village aimed at tourists is being developed at Parque da Floresta. The village overlooks the front nine holes of the course. On average, real estate prices at Parque da Floresta have more than doubled each 10 of the last 20 years. According to the developers, Vigia Group, the new development is ideally suited to satisfy the strong demand for the golf and holiday rental market.

Prices start at $412,000 for townhouses and $593,000 for villas. Corporate & Commercial, a specialist British property-finance broker, are offering a package tailored to prospective investors. Based on an independent bank valuation of the properties, investors will be offered loans of up to 85% of the property price, coupled with a discount on multiple purchases. The interest rate is one to two points above the prevailing three-month bank rate.

Vigia offers guaranteed returns after the completion of the development, estimated to be in five years. At this time, it is anticipated the resort will be sufficiently established to meet the high standards required by international tour operators. The Vigia Group is prepared to offer a five-year rental contract. That's not to say income cannot be generated through ad-hoc rentals in the meantime, but it won't be guaranteed. Over the five years, average annual income for a two-bedroom townhouse at Quinta da Encosta Velha is estimated at $14,400. See *www.parquedafloresta.com* for details.

Renting

Finding long-term rentals on the Algarve can be tricky. As they can get higher returns, owners prefer to let by the week to holiday makers. However, long winter lets abound with most one-bedroom furnished apartments going from $550 to $700 per month from October to Easter. The rent often includes utility charges. Even short-term rentals can be very reasonable. I met three British seniors staying in Praia da Rocha for seven weeks. Their furnished apartment cost an equivalent $20 per day ...including utilities.

To rent an Algarve villa long-term over the winter months, expect to pay at least $1,000 per month—more for quality properties. Through *www.central-algarve.com*, $1,800 monthly is the going winter rate for a three-bedroom furnished villa with pool at Valverde. For $1,080 monthly, it also lists a two-bedroom, two-bathroom townhouse at Vale do Lobo. With sea views and a sun terrace, it's within easy walking distance of the beach and Vale do Lobo central square. This property is normally rented by the week: from $850 a month in the low season to $1,820 in August. At those rates, you can understand why owners prefer short-term vacation lets.

Lisbon's rental mix is approximately 50% furnished, 50% unfurnished. Leases run for at least six months, generally a year. Usual terms are two months' advance rent for unfurnished apartments, and three months for furnished.

Sample apartment rental prices in Lisbon

• Calcada da Ajuda—860-square-foot apartment in a traditional-style house, $660 monthly.

• Benfica—860 square feet, $720.

• Lapa—1,075 square feet, $990.

• Expo—1,200 square feet, $1,080.

• Belem—967 square feet, $1,200. This Lisbon seaside neighborhood is the site of the white wedding-cake monastery of Jeronimos, where Vasco da Gama is buried.

• Chiado—1,342 square feet in a building dating from 1900, $1200. The Chiado is a very chic central Lisbon neighborhood with quality shops and cafés.

On the Lisbon coast, Rentavila's Cascais agency has a selection of furnished rentals, but most agents can find you something. One-bedroom furnished apartments start at around $660 monthly, though at the less expensive end of the scale, you're unlikely to have a sea view. As always, the better the location, the more you pay. A

970-square-foot apartment in the center of Estoril, in a condominium with swimming pool and closed garage, and only minutes away from the station, beach, etc., is $1,620 monthly. A 1,400-square-foot family house in the center of Cascais with large garden and garage is $2,400 monthly.

A lease agreement between you and the landlord is drawn up by a notary. The agreement will state the amount of rent and when it is payable, the contents of the property, length of contract, etc. The minimum period for a long-term rental is generally a year, but in well-known holiday areas, three- or six-month leases are common.

Rents are payable in advance, either monthly or quarterly. Contracts generally include a requirement for a security deposit—generally one month's rent—to cover any possible damage.

In most instances, the landlord is normally responsible for paying the annual property taxes; tenants are liable for utility bills. (Though this isn't always the case for winter lets on the Algarve.) In some apartment complexes, you may also be liable for service charges. The rent may or may not cover them, but the contract should state who is liable for these charges.

What potential buyers should know

What's a T2? At first sight, Portuguese listings look baffling. However, cracking the code is easy once you know that this is realtors' shorthand for how many bedrooms an apartment has. A T0 is a studio, a T1 is a one-bedroom apartment, a T2 is a two-bedroom apartment, and so on.

You want to build your own home? Don't be tempted to buy "rural land" without planning permission, certainly if a structure or ruin doesn't already exist. The land may be completely useless for your purposes as building laws have become very restrictive. Especially on the Algarve, any plots with ruins sell for astonishing sums. At Ferrarias, a couple of miles inland from Albufeira, a tiny plot (2,550 square feet) with approval for a project is $164,600.

Even where ruins exist, be careful. Planners rarely allow anything that's more than 10% larger than the original structure—so constructing your dream home may not be feasible. Costs start at around $85 per square foot, but that's not luxury level. The price also depends on the builder. One agent says a 2,000-square-foot villa would cost more like $250,000 to build—and that's on top of the cost of the land.

You can't build willy-nilly, and though that can be a good thing, it often leads to frustration. I was told of one couple who waited two years to get permission from the *camara* (municipal council) to install a swimming pool.

Beware of offshore ownership

You may have heard that you can save around 10% of your purchase costs by setting up an offshore company to buy Portuguese property. It's estimated that 75% of foreigners currently own homes here via offshore companies. When a property is held offshore, buyers aren't really purchasing a property, but shares in a company that owns the property. These buyers can avoid property-transfer fees (SISA), taxes, as well as the legal, notary, and registration charges that are usually levied on the purchase of properties—obviously an attractive arrangement.

But hang fire on going down this route for the moment. Some nasty changes are afoot...

The *Reforma do Patrimonio* came into force in January 2004 with the intention of reforming Portugal's property legislation. Any property owned by an offshore company will now be forced to pay an annual charge of 5% of the property's value if the company is registered anywhere other than Malta, Delaware, or New Zealand.

Under this new legislation, anybody owning a house valued at $700,000 will be faced with an annual $35,000 tax bill if they decide to retain ownership in a non-acceptable tax haven.

Owners who bought through an offshore company now basically have three options. First, they can sell. Second, they can transfer ownership of the offshore company to an acceptable location—at an estimated cost of approximately $8,500. Third, they can pay capital gains tax and a purchase tax to bring the property onshore.

Britain's *Sunday Times* reported the case of one aggrieved man who paid $430,000 for a villa that's now worth around $1.7 million. To convert the ownership from an offshore company to an onshore company is likely to cost him dear. According to the newspaper, the total bill —including capital gains tax, legal and notary fees—will come to about $412,800...just to stay living in a property that he already owns.

Buying your home

For most non-offshore buyers, additional purchase costs currently amount to around 12%, but this is set to fall to around 10%. SISA (property purchase tax), varies according to property value.

Under the new property laws, SISA isn't levied on homes under $96,000. For more valuable properties over $600,000, it has been reduced from a maximum of 10% down to 6% for urban dwellings, and to 5% for rural homes. Between the $96,000 and $600,000 bands, a graduated scale of rates applies.

Notary and registration fees are approximately 2% to 2.5% of the purchase price. In Portugal, estate agent's fees are normally paid by the vendor, not the buyer.

It's acceptable to make an offer on a property. Around 10% can sometimes be shaved off the asking price. However, much depends on an area's desirability...for a rare T1 (one-bedroom apartment) in Lisbon's Lapa neighborhood, the vendor certainly won't haggle like a Turkish trinket trader.

After agreeing on a price, appoint a lawyer to check legal and title issues. You might also get the help of a surveyor. Lawyer's fees are around 2%. Surveyors charge in the region of $700 to $1500. Normal procedure is to pay a 10% deposit on signing the *contrato promesso,* the preliminary contract. If buyers fail to complete without just cause, their deposit is forfeited; if vendors withdraw, they are liable to pay you double the deposit. Transferring ownership normally takes four to eight weeks.

Before signing the final *escritura* contract, you need to import the necessary funds to buy the property along with associated taxes and legal fees. As proof of ownership, the *escritura* must be filed with the Land Registry, and with Portugal's tax authorities. Prior to buying a property, you must also apply for a fiscal number.

Residency permits

If you intend to stay in Portugal for more than 90 days, you'll need to apply to the Portuguese embassy for a "Type 1" residence visa. These are initially valid for a period of 180 days. To further extend your stay, you'll then need to contact the nearest office of the immigration authorities (*Serviço de Estrangeiros e Fronteras*) and apply for a residency permit.

- **Embassy of Portugal,** *2125 Kalorama Road, NW, Washington, D.C. 20008; tel. (202)328-8610; e-mail: portugal@portugalemb.org.*

Cost of ownership

Annual property taxes are based on the taxable value of a property —and many older Portuguese homes have not been revalued for years. Under Portugal's new property legislation, there is to be wholesale revaluation, and any property changing hands will automatically be revalued. The Portuguese Valuation Commissioners advise that new taxable values are likely to be between 80% and 90% of a property's market value.

Each local authority sets its own charge, currently 0.8% to 1.2%. This is set to fall to 0.2% to 0.5% of a property's taxable value. But until revaluation occurs (the government forecasts a five-year transition period) a rate of between 0.4% to 0.8% of the corrected taxable value will be levied on existing property owners, with a yearly ceiling on increases until 2008.

But you're a new buyer, so say you've purchased a home for $250,000 and the Valuation Commissioners give it a taxable value of $220,000. Depending on where the property is situated, annual property taxes will be between $440 and $1,100.

For a $150,000 apartment (taxable value $125,000), annual property taxes will be somewhere between $250 and $625.

An apartment in a residence attracts condo charges. These can be as low as $300 annually, but that's bottom-end. Expect higher charges for facilities like communal pools, tennis courts, and large gardens —probably $1000 to $1,500 a year for a typical two-bedroom apartment. Some condos charge an amount per bedroom—one development near Albufeira in the Algarve quotes $750 per bedroom.

Cost of living

In most parts of Portugal, $15,000 per year should cover mid-range expenditures for two people. This takes in general maintenance of a home, property taxes, electricity, heating, telephone, etc., as well as automobile expenses, groceries, entertainment, and dining at local restaurants twice a week.

Obviously much depends on the type of property you buy—and your own lifestyle. The upper end of the market can be very pricey. Running costs for a three-bedroom villa with private pool on a luxury Algarve development can be over $8,000 per year for bills, communal charges, annual taxes, swimming pool and garden maintenance, and repair work. For palatial homes, the annual total comes in at more like $13,000.

However, smaller seaside apartments or cottages in inland areas won't require anything like that.

Average annual housing expenses in Portugal
Property taxes—$500 annually.
Apartment service charges—$1,500 annually.
Water—around $170 (including water rates of $62) annually.
Gas for cooking—$18 a bottle, which lasts two months.
Electricity—around $432 annually or $36 per month.
A ton of wood for winter heating if your house or cottage has a wood-burning stove—$130.

Eating out in Portugal is cheap. Many places offer three-course set menus—with house wine—for under $10. Sometimes a menu can be as low as $6 which makes it feel like it's as cheap to eat out as eat in. Groceries cost around 35% less than in northern European countries —you can get pork chops for $2.60 per pound and oranges for 21 cents per pound.

North Americans need private medical insurance, but facilities are considered good in both public and private sectors. Hospitals at Faro, Albufeira, Portimao, and Lagos all have English-speaking doctors. A visit to a private doctor will cost around $60, sometimes less—popular resorts also have medical centers with English-speaking staff. Luzdoc, a private clinic in Praia da Luz, charges $54 for a weekday consultation. I spoke to an English lady who had needed X-rays ($2.10) and a course of painkillers ($33).

Paying your taxes

An individual is considered to be a resident of Portugal if he/she spends more than 183 days per calendar year in the country. If you are deemed to be a resident, then your worldwide income is subject to tax within Portugal. If you're non-resident, then only your income from Portuguese sources is of concern to the Portuguese taxman.

Non-residents must make an annual return for income tax if they receive income from letting property. For non-residents, income on rental profits is taxable at a flat rate of 25%. You may be liable for wealth tax, capital gains tax, and inheritance tax. Individual situations vary and it is best to seek specialist advice from a tax consultant who has knowledge of both the U.S. and Portuguese tax systems.

If you decide to become a resident of Portugal, rental income is added to any other income you may have. After allowances, your total income is then taxed on a sliding scale.

Portuguese income tax rates
Up to $4,920—12%
$4,920 to $7,440—14%
$7,440 to $18,450—24%
$18,450 to $42,435—34%
$42,435 to $61,501—38%
Above $61,501—40%

When you decide to sell

When the proceeds of a property sale are reinvested into other permanent assets (another Portuguese property or shares, etc.), only 20% of capital gains tax need be paid in the current year. The balance is deferred to the following years.

If it's your primary residence (and you're considered a resident of Portugal for tax purposes), 50% of the gain is added to your regular income for income tax purposes. If the proceeds are invested in the purchase of another primary residence within two years, the capital gain is exempt from tax.

For non-residents who sell their property, the capital gains tax is levied at 25% of the gain.

Chapter 7

Spain

Picture a sun-drenched, white house with a shady courtyard, perched on top of a cliff in southern Spain. With the deep blue sea beyond and an olive grove nestling nearby, it's the stuff of which fantasies are made.

Beaches...mountains...fabulous cities...cracking festivals. And, of course, guaranteed sunshine. It's not surprising that southern Spain is the most popular country for Europeans seeking a home overseas.

Despite what you may have heard, there's far more to Spain than golf courses and the concrete sprawl of look-alike apartments. (Though it must be said that concrete features highly in many of the resorts in popular package tours.)

Just venture a few miles into the Andalucian hinterland...into the far west...along the Bay of Biscay...along the Costa de la Luz and Costa Azahar. "The real Spain" is waiting for you. Almost unknown territory to foreign tourists, here mountain foothills are strung with citrus groves and villages cling to a centuries-old way of life.

But if you prefer modern comforts to rural simplicity, the Costa Blanca and Costa del Sol regions of Spain's Mediterranean coast are among Europe's best investment bets. Such is the appeal of places like Marbella that the price of a home bought off-plan is often considerably more—around 30%—once completed. Many people buy and sell solely for that reason.

How much for a home in Spain? Well, there's a huge price variation across the 17 regions...and also from town to town within the regions. But while property prices have almost doubled in the past four years, it's still possible to unearth village houses and small coastal apartments for under $100,000. Look to regions like the Costa Azahar (Orange Blossom Coast) and it's possible to find bargains such as 880-square-foot apartments for $72,000 and three-bedroom townhouses for $139,000.

But do take your time when shopping for a property. Some properties sell within a month, but others can linger on the market for a year —often because owners are seeking unrealistic sums.

To give you a ballpark figure, at the moment this is how things stand in Spain as a whole:

- Average square-foot price for new homes—$152 (up 12% in the past year)

- Average square-foot price for resales—$128 (up 18% in the past year)

Average prices of modern homes

The average price that buyers are paying for a modern homes with 1,200 to 1,400 square feet of living space vary widely by region.

- Rural Spain—$132,000.
- Costa de la Luz—$168,000.
- Costa Brava—$228,000.
- Costa Blanca—$216,000 to $276,000 (north of Alicante is the most expensive)
- Costa del Sol—$252,000 to $480,000 (Malaga to Marbella is the most expensive)
- Majorca and Ibiza—$480,000.

Average prices for apartments

- Madrid—$270 per square foot. Prime locations such as Salamanca, $560 to $670. For a 1,075-square-foot apartment, $290,000 to $558,000, and up.

- Bilbao and San Sebastian—$223 per square foot. Prime locations, $670. For a 1,075-square-foot apartment, $240,000 to $720,000.

- Barcelona—$220 per square foot. Prime locations: $560. For a 1,075-square-foot apartment, $237,000 to $500,000, and up.

- Santander (Cantabria)—$160 per square foot. Prime locations: $390 to $470. For a 1,075-square-foot apartment, $173,000 to $505,000.

- Seville—$125 per square foot. For a 1,075-square-foot apartment, $136,000 and up.

- Cádiz—$116 per square foot. For a 1,075-square-foot apartment, $125,000 and up.

- Valencia—$98 per square foot. For a 1,075-square-foot apartment, $105,000 and up.

Barcelona

There's something electric about port cities...and Barcelona is definitely high voltage. Spain's spruced-up second city has a 24-hour lifestyle and is popular for weekend breaks with Europeans. They come to meander down Las Ramblas with its bird sellers and all-night newsstands; sip *cava* (Catalan champagne) in the Café de l'Opera; climb the mosaic towers of Gaudi's temple, the Sagrada Familia; wander the Bario Gotic's twisty streets; eat $10 *menu del dias* in fish restaurants in working-class Barceloneta.

While it's a wonderful city in which to live or invest—there are some splendid residences with high ceilings and parquet floors— prices are steep in central areas. In the Poble Sec neighborhood, near Las Ramblas, the asking price for a 750-square-foot apartment in a refurbished building dating from 1910 is $294,000. In the Eixample neighborhood near the Sagrada Familia cathedral, VDH Enterprises also has a 750-square-foot apartment with access to private garden for $248,000, but it needs refurbishing at an additional cost of around $42,000.

The neighborhood of Graca is becoming fashionable among arty types, but still retains its pleasingly old-fashioned air. But even here, a move-into-tomorrow studio apartment (540 square feet) in a good building can fetch $250,000.

- **Van den Hout Enterprises**, *Carrer Arago 463, Pral 7a, 08013 Barcelona; tel. (34)93-265-35-15; e-mail: office@vdhenterprises.com; website: www.vdhenterprises.com.*

The Costa Brava

Wedged between the snow-capped Pyrenees and the Mediterranean, the picture-book province of Catalunya boasts Spain's most spectacular coastal scenery—the Costa Brava. The name means "Wild Coast," and it's a ruggedly beautiful place of pine-covered cliffs and secret coves. The Catalan countryside has its own special magic, too ...tranquil green lanes overhung with trees, medieval villages crowned with ancient citadels, and centuries-old farmhouses lying in the folds of the hills.

Although not virgin territory, Catalunya usually gets overlooked in the stampede to the southern Costas. Few people stumble across the exquisite harbor villages around Cap de Begur. Llafranc, Aguia Blava, Sa Tuna, Tamariu—all are unsullied by mass tourism. Tucked inside coves of rosy pink rocks, they're the Costa Brava's hidden gems. Gold, green, and turquoise...the seascapes are absolutely gorgeous. Brightly colored boats pack miniature harbors, beaches form perfect golden crescents, and the aquamarine waters are transparently crystal-clear.

Llafranc and Tamariu are intimate harbor villages with small clusters of whitewashed *residencia* apartments climbing the pine-clad hills. Both have golden arcs of sandy beach, tree-shaded promenades dotted with terraced cafés and coastal paths. During winter, the upturned sailing boats beached on its strand look just like a school of miniature whales. For a two-storey Tamariu villa with pool and vistas of the sea and mountains, the asking price is $408,000.

Begur is the best place to start looking for properties around Llafranc and neighboring villages. Three miles from Aigua Blava on the coast, this medieval hilltop town has wonderful views of a splendid castle and the sea from its *mirador* on Placa Forgas. If Begur takes your fancy, a pretty house—modern, around 1,610 square feet and within walking distance of town—is $432,000 through Domus. In the surrounding *urbanizations* (suburbs), it also lists homes with around 1,075 square feet of living space from $198,000 to $264,000.

Don't expect many bargains on the coast either—you'll pay a premium for such stunning locations. Three hundred yards from the beach at Cap Rubi, an 805-square-foot apartment in a residence with a pool is $324,600. With magnificent sea views at Aiguablava, a duplex with 1,160 square feet of living space is $384,000.

Another likeable part of the Costa Brava is Palamos and its satellite villages of Sa Forsa and Sant Antoni de Calonge. This is more south central—just over an hour away on the *autopista* (highway), Barcelona is within easy commuting distance. Palamos is a small town with a working port, evening fish market—and a housing market that's mostly local.

In the hills above, toward the medieval village of Calonge, there are some lovely villas with red pantiled roofs. Views are fabulous and some villas have traditional Catalan features like round rooftop towers. For a villa with private pool, 1,230 square feet of living space and additional terraces, prices start at around $390,000. On a development in nearby Santa Caterina, VDH Enterprises in Barcelona has a 2,150-square-foot villa for $356,000.

Imposing stone-built *masias* (Catalan country farmhouses) have become very expensive. They're huge, usually 4,500 square feet or more, but a fully restored full-size masia with pool and 2 to 3 acres of land usually fetches at least $1 million if it's anywhere near the coast. Domus, however, has a *masia* near Palafrugell for $900,000. Further back in the countryside toward Girona, the real estate agent also has a couple to restore for $384,000 and $420,000. On 2 acres, the latter is at Sant Joan de Palamos and will yield living space of almost 6,500 square feet.

- **Agencia de Serveis Immobiliaris Domus,** *Creu 23, Begur, 17255 Girona; tel. (34)972-622-072. e-mail: domus@domusbegur.com; website: www.domusbegur.com.*

The Costa del Sol

For Europeans, the Costa del Sol is the most popular part of the Spanish coastline to buy, rent, or invest. Part of Andalucia province, its infrastructure is excellent: there are international schools, first-class medical facilities—and there's certainly no problem finding real estate agents, doctors, and lawyers who speak English.

But for North Americans looking to immerse themselves in Spanish culture, it might not have the same appeal as it holds for sunshine-seeking British, Germans, and Scandinavians. The region has exclusive areas such as the smart marina resort of Puerto Banus, but it encompasses the high-rise horrors of Torremolinos too. Many coastal resorts feel as Spanish as Manchester or Munich

There's no getting away from the fact that the Costa del Sol is over-built—and much of it is overpriced too. Location is everything here. Whether it's beachfront or in the foothills, there's a huge variation in prices.

There's little point in shopping with less than $100,000. While you can find the odd small apartment for less, it'll be in older, undesireable concrete blocks—or hold as much space as a dollhouse. In the central zone, between Fuengirola and Marbella, at a development with communal pool at La Cala, $95,800 is sought for a teeny studio of just 320 square feet. Think that's ludicrously expensive? For a studio the same size in a good part of Marbella, you'll pay $167,800.

Golf property almost matches beachfront apartments as the top seller in Spain's property boom. Those who purchase golf property as an investment usually rent their property for most of the year. Returns can be around 8% to 10%. Real estate agents or the golf complex developer will arrange to manage the rentals for a fee of around 15%.

Property on new golf courses is usually purchased off-plan before construction begins. Off-plan purchasers get a good initial price, because you're effectively financing the developer by putting money down before the property is finished. Depending on the project, you can usually expect returns of 20% to 30% on your money if you resell within a year.

If you're seeking a golf property, La Cala Golf Resort has a new project called Los Altos. Two-bedroom apartments are $324,000 and three-bedroom apartments cost $504,000. Purchase includes membership of La Cala Golf Club, where a third 18-hole course will open in 2004. A townhouse development here is in the pipeline, as well as a number of other projects. Plans are for 1,000 units to be built around its golf courses.

Marbella is a huge favorite with foreign buyers. A new highway now means it's only a mere 30-minute drive from Malaga's international airport. An average new property with two bedrooms in an apartment building now costs $290,000; the average villa costs $466,000.

The Marbella municipal area is huge. As it takes in a lot of neighborhoods, you'll almost certainly find properties at prices below the notional average. For example, a 1,074-square-foot individual villa in a development with a communal pool in Marbella East is $360,000. Although it has distant sea views and is in excellent decorative order, the likely reason why it's below the average is that it was built in 1978. And "villas" at that price level are little more than ordinary bungalows or townhouses.

In Nueva Andalucia (Marbella West), the starting price for a "small and cozy" villa is $230,000. Built in 1975, it's definitely small and it's definitely cozy—for this price you get a mere 805 square feet of living space plus a terrace of 320 square feet. However, this home is in a quiet corner of Nueva Andalucia, but still close to La Campana, a popular area of bars and restaurants. Plus it's only a five-minutes drive from Puerto Banus and close to La Quinta, Los Naranjos, and Las Brisas golf courses. From its elevated position, the house offers sea views.

At posh Puerto Banus, you could buy a 700-square-foot apartment for $250,000—but in a really top-quality residence with a pool, you could spend $330,000 for just 535 square feet of living space. Apartments of 1,075 square feet start at $336,000—and go upward from there.

There is a phenomenal number of real estate agencies on the Costa del Sol. The website portal *www.andalucia.com* has links to dozens. One of the largest is Ocean Estates.

- **Ocean Estates,** *Avda Julio Iglesias 3, Puerto Banus, 29660 Marbella, Malaga; tel.(34)952-811-750; e-mail: info@oceanestates.com; website: www.oceanestates.com.*

Beyond the Costa—rural Andalucia

For a taste of a more authentic Spain, the hills behind the Costa del Sol's busy resorts and golf course condominiums turn up plenty of options. Here you'll find centuries-old whitewashed villages—the famous *pueblos blancos*. Steeped in the remains of their Moorish past, they cling like limpets to the steep hillsides.

It's magical to go house hunting in the 30 or so towns and villages of the mountainous Axarquia area, high in the foothills above Malaga. No mass tourism, no high-rise hotels. Instead, you find a timeless landscape of orange groves and avocado pear plantations, where mules and oxen remain in daily use.

Images of Andalucia, a real estate agent, specializes in property for sale in this area. Its portfolio includes everything from habitable village houses starting at $86,000, to handsome *cortijos* (traditional farmhouses built around a courtyard) from $159,000. Country cottages begin at around the $97,000 mark—and if you're seeking something really unusual, how about a cave? Almost unique within Western Europe, people in the hills beyond Granada have been making use of caves for centuries. Fifty minutes from the coast, Images of Andalucia currently has a cave home for $108,000.

- **Images of Andalucia,** *Cortijo del Roble, Carboneras, 29312 Villanueva del Rosario (Malaga); tel./fax (34)952-111-178; e-mail: use form on website; website www.imagesofandalucia.com.*

Andalucia's alternative coast—the Costa de la Luz

Andalucia is actually more sizeable than some countries. Most people usually think the province and the Costa del Sol are the same thing, but there's a lot more to Andalucia than endless resorts. It's divided into eight provinces: Malaga, Seville, Cordoba, Granada, Jaen, Almeria, Huelva, and Cádiz.

Fringing Cádiz and Huelva provinces, the Costa de la Luz is Andalucia's Atlantic coast. Divided from the Mediterranean by the Rock of Gibraltar, "The Coast of Light" has plenty going for it: 3,000 annual sunshine hours...over 125 miles of golden-white beaches...and an almost unbelievable clarity of light. Excellent sports facilities include horseback riding, deep-sea fishing, and golf.

Care is being taken to protect this undiscovered region, nicknamed "the Spanish Algarve" because of its proximity to the Portuguese border. A property here could be a very worthwhile investment—homes are substantially cheaper than equivalent properties on both the Costa del Sol and the Portuguese Algarve. Plus, strict planning laws mean that it will never become overbuilt.

A good town for a property search in Costa de la Luz is Chiclana de la Frontera. Splendid beaches are just seven miles away and settlements near Playa La Barrosa are some of Spain's most architecturally charming. Small, low-rise apartments and intensely white, attached houses with neat, flowery gardens front the beach. In the pine woods beyond are low-density developments—apartments and individual bungalows, usually set around a communal swimming pool.

La Barrosa's golden sands run for five miles down to Novo Sancti Petri where there's a golf course. Even in winter these little resorts aren't dead—most beachfront cafés remain open and there are plenty of people about.

With views to the salt marshes, Los Gallos is a quiet residential area between Chiclana town and the coast (La Barrosa), only a four-minute drive in each direction. It has a commercial center, big supermarket, bars, restaurants, and other amenities. Being sold furnished, a two-bedroom apartment in a residence with a communal pool and tennis court is $104,000.

Agencia Luz Atlantic also has a good selection of modern three-bedroom bungalows in the Chiclana area for between $155,000 and $177,000. There's a price tag of $166,000 on a 1,180-square-foot bungalow in Pago Melilla, a rural residential area surrounded by pine trees.

Only three minutes' driving time to the beach, this neighborhood is next door to Novo Sancti Petri, one of Chiclana's most exclusive residential areas with golf courses, hotels, and a good choice of bars and restaurants. The property has three bedrooms, en-suite bathroom, shower room, fully fitted kitchen with exit to the back garden, and living room with fireplace and terrace.

As holiday lets, most two-bedroom apartments rent for $215 weekly off-season, rising to $1,300 to $1,800 for a minimum of two weeks in August. Depending on the area, a three-bedroom bungalow will rent for $1,200 to $1,600 for two weeks in July and August. In luxury developments such as Roche, owners are asking rental prices of $3,000 to $3,600 for two weeks in high summer. A 2,150-square-foot villa with a pool here will cost you in the region of $595,000.

Further along the coast, Conil de la Frontera has nine miles of wide, gently shelving beaches and small golden coves sheltering below sandstone cliffs. There are two suggestions about how Conil got its name. Some say it's from an Arabic word meaning "a place of delight," others insist it's to do with rabbits—the pinewoods are jumping with bunnies.

About 17,000 people live in the area and various festivals take place throughout the year. One traditional event is the annual Fiesta of the Virgen del Carmen on July 16, when fishermen take a statue of the Madonna to sea.

Small *urbanizacions* have been built at nearby La Palmera, Roche, Fontanilla, and Fuente del Gallo, where apartments and small detached bungalows carry similar prices to those in Chiclana. Remember that extremely bijou studio in Marbella for $167,800? Here you have a slightly larger one (375 square feet) for $57,700. Through Rio Salado, a whitewashed village house with five small bedrooms and two bathrooms seems a steal at $122,600.

- **Agencia Luz Atlantic,** *Residencial Almadraba Manzana 4-N3, 11130 Chiclana de la Fra., Cádiz; tel. (34)956-537-240; e-mail: info@Cádiz-costaluz.com; website www.Cádiz-costa-luz.com.*

• **Rio Salado,** *La Gaviota, Calle Laguna 16-1 F, Conil de la Frontera; tel. (34)956- 456-080; e-mail: info@inmoconil.com; website: www. inmoconil.com.*

The White Villages

Beyond the Cádiz coastline lies more magic...a realm of lonely marshes, pink flamingos, and salt pans glittering in the sunlight. Follow the *Ruta de los Pueblos Blancos* (Route of the White Villages) and you'll come across dazzlingly white settlements swarming atop crumpled hills. Some villages are little changed since medieval times.

"White Villages" are becoming more in demand, both for their individuality and value for money. Prices are increasing due to scarcity. Whether you're seeking a holiday or permanent home, or simply to invest, now is a good time to buy.

Two charming villages are Arcos de la Frontera and Vejer de la Frontera. The words *de la Frontera* after many place names hereabouts indicate that long ago they were border towns between Christian and Muslim Spain. Throughout the early Middle Ages, Andalucia was a Moorish kingdom and it wasn't until the 12th century that Spain's Christian rulers started making serious attempts to wrest back the peninsula. A number of white villages played a major role in the *Reconquista,* the struggle that ended with Granada's fall in 1492.

Midway between Cádiz and Seville, Arcos de la Frontera was one of the first settlements captured by the Moors. It didn't return to Spanish rule until 1255. Crowned by a castle, it perches on a sheer cliff, a dizzying plunge that nature could have specifically designed to repel invaders. The town's oldest part is full of alleys that twist past convents, balconied mansions, and little white houses. Many are guarded by grilled windows and wrought-iron gateways opening onto tiled patios, often with small fountains in the middle. Vejer is an equally atmospheric place of tangled lanes, narrow stone stairways, and hideouts for sleeping cats.

Renovated houses of around 1,400 square feet (three bedrooms, salon, bathroom, kitchen, terrace, and sometimes a gorgeous tiled patio) normally go for between $150,000 and $340,000 in these villages. Cottages still needing work can be had for $115,000. If you're seeking a restoration project, the phrase is *no reformada* (not renovated). Apartments in restored buildings (500 to 650 square feet) cost $47,000 to $70,000; more sizeable apartments, say 700 to 1,000 square feet, fetch $68,000 to $125,000. Or you could rent. Two-bedroom homes average $450 monthly on a one-year lease.

Jimena de la Frontera is a little cheaper. It's at the foot of Ronda Sierras, 40 minutes inland from Gibraltar and 30 minutes from Sotogrande on the Costa del Sol. Originally a Roman settlement, most houses for sale here are terraced and come in various shapes and sizes. Unrenovated houses are $36,000 to $132,000 depending on condition and size.

Houses that have already been converted cost from $45,000 to $220,000, again depending on size and standard. Most houses are at least 200 years old and are (or could be) a delightful mixture of old beamed ceilings, sunny patios, and all the conveniences for modern living.

For Jimena's residents, it's not exactly back to the medieval. The village has a swimming pool, gym, banks, shops, supermarkets, and a well-equipped health center. For the more culture vulture, there are art galleries...painting and pottery classes...flamenco evenings...music festivals. The village also has its own resident masseuse and acupuncturist. Or, explore the area's castle ruins and surrounding countryside (known as a haven for a wide variety of birds). Go by foot or horseback. You can hire a horse at the town's riding stables.

- **Venasierra,** *'Cerro de la Reina' nivel 1—no 15, 11630 Arcos de la Frontera (Cádiz); tel. (34)956-700-109; e-mail: venasierra@ venasierra.com; website www.venasierra.com.*

- **La Segur Agencia,** *Nuestra Senora de la Oliva 19, 1150 Vejer de la Frontera (Cádiz); tel. (34)956-451-082; e-mail: lasegur@wanadoo.es.*

- **Miles of Andalucia Inmobiliaria,** *Avenida de los Deportes 3, 11330 Jimena de la Frontera, Cádiz; tel. (34)956-641-198; e-mail: andaluciamiles@spainsouth.com; website www.spainsouth.com/miles.*

City life—Cádiz

The city serving the Costa de la Luz is Cádiz. One of the oldest maritime cities in Europe, its history goes back to the time of the Phoenicians. Street names such as Trinidad, Venezuela, Honduras, and Argentina conjure up the glory days when Spain ruled the oceans. One of Columbus's ships, the *Santa Maria*, was fitted out a few miles away at Puerto de Santa Maria.

A university and port city with a population of 155,000, today's Cádiz is a buzzing workplace, oozing shabby chic. The five-mile-long new quarter of modern apartment buildings and shopping areas is flanked by a wide promenade of palm trees and three golden beaches: Playa de Santa Maria del Mar, Playa de la Victoria, and Playa de Cortadura. Although the "average" for a 1,075-square-foot apartment in Cádiz is $125,000, in this part of the city you'll pay more like $196,000 for one with views of the bay.

Within Old Cádiz's walls, a warren of skinny lanes snake around the old watchtowers and a cathedral domed with mustard-colored tiles. Come evening, shopkeepers awaken from the afternoon siesta, flower sellers re-emerge onto Plaza de Topete, and bars seethe with chat and laughter. Tucked in beside tiny chapels, most shops are hole-in-the-wall places. Men in overalls buy car parts...old ladies indulge in sticky sweets and pastries...kids press their noses up against the glass to see tumbling puppy dogs in the pet shop. Here a display of wigs...there a tiny shop selling knitting wool...next door a bar-cum-butcher's shop where you can sample slices of sausage or smoked Iberian ham with a glass of salty *manzanilla* sherry...

The best place to buy in old Cádiz is around the seafront Alameda gardens or on one of the sunny plazas. Further into the warren, little light penetrates down some calles. Even four-storey buildings sometimes seem too tall. Many houses have admittedly fallen into a flaky state but signs of rejuvenation are under way. A number have already been being transformed into new apartments; many more dilapidated mansions are being converted. One-bedroom apartments (550 square feet) in restored buildings start at $72,000. Through Mundocasa, a 645-

square-foot apartment in the Juan de Dios barrio near the Cathedral is $104,000. However, you can pay a lot more. A refurbished 1,400-square-foot apartment in a building with a stunning inner courtyard is $295,800.

- **Mundocasa Gestion Inmobiliaria,** *Plaza de San Juan de Dios 3, 11006 Cádiz; tel. (34)956-266-560.*

English-speaking realtors are thin on the ground in Cádiz. If you're interested in buying here and need English-speaking help, try working your way through listings in Tucasa (a free local property magazine) or its website at *www.tucasa.com.*

The Costa Blanca

Less commercialized than the Costa del Sol, the Costa Blanca (White Coast) is the second most popular choice for foreign buyers seeking retirement or holiday homes. Over 100,000 British buyers now own property here, and there are considerable numbers of German, Dutch, and Scandinavian residents, too.

The 132 mile-long coastline features over 60 miles of golden sandy beaches and coves. Set against a backdrop of wooded sierras that turn pink at sunset, most resorts are clean and well-kept. Studded with marinas, bars, cafés, and delectable seafood restaurants, its seafront promenades are perfect for long, leisurely strolls.

Rock climbing...trekking...horseback riding...rambling. Patrolled by birds of prey, the rural hinterland also offers up ancient monasteries, vineyards, and a succession of little towns and villages set among orange, lemon, and almond groves.

Although the 1960s building frenzy resulted in some awful architectural mistakes, the Costa Blanca isn't all wall-to-wall monolithic blocks. Along much of the coastline, you can still glimpse the Mediterranean. The mega-resort of Benidorm is a notorious exception, but big gaps remain between most seaside towns.

According to the World Health Organization, the Costa Blanca enjoys one of the world's healthiest climates, especially if you suffer from rheumatism or arthritis. Winters aren't as cold or wet as the Costa Brava, and summers are nowhere near as hot and humid as on the Costa del Sol. On average, you can expect 30 days of rain, 15 days of cloud cover, and 320 days of sunny blue skies. The temperature in January averages 51° F, 57° F in March, 68° F in May, 80° F in August, and 59° F in November.

All kinds of properties for all kinds of buyers...and at all kinds of prices. Starting figure is around $72,000 for a bolthole of a studio for vacations, and $165,000 for a two-storey terraced bungalow of 925 square feet. While you can easily pay $432,000 for a 2,000-square-foot villa with terraces and pool, that's still substantially less than on most parts of the Costa del Sol. Spectacular views obviously push up prices, though.

Traditional village homes and townhouses are less popular than apartments, villas, and "urbanizations." Those are basically houses in a development—Spanish suburbia, if you like. Some homes are exclusive, others are identikit little boxes with whitewashed walls and russet-tiled roofs. Nothing to distress most people's aesthetic sensibilities, but they can seem rather bland. For the budget-minded, two of the most afford-able urbanization areas are Denia's Las Marinas and Cumbre del Sol, a vast urbanization south of Javea.

Most newer apartments are in low-rise residences with lush gardens, tennis courts, and swimming pools. On the other hand, the oldest developments—basically designed for vacation apartments —sometimes resemble a correctional facility. Small studio apartments are advertised for as low as $34,000, but I doubt you'd be tempted.

If you're considering investment property, annual returns on the Costa Blanca are around 5% to 6% net. The most lettable properties are those that aren't too far from an airport, close to the beach, and are also golf and marina properties. New (or nearly new) apartments in quality residences with a pool are considered to have good investment potential: two-bedroom units are the most sought after. Here's one "investment" example: a 1,200-square-foot apartment in a residence with a communal pool close to Altea town for $203,500.

Costa Blanca resort sampler

Flanked by over seven miles of sandy beaches on one side, and rocky rust-colored coves on the other, Denia (population 28,500) hasn't lost its Spanish identity. Topped by an old castle, and fronted by seafood restaurants, streets behind the harbor are lined with cottages in a painter's palette of cobalt blue, salmon-pink, mossy green, bright tangerine, and primrose. Many have a songbird in a little cage outside the front door. In this Fisherman's Quarter, you can buy a restored cottage of 1,075 square feet for $119,000.

There's ample opportunity for long, healthy walks. You can amble for almost three miles from Las Rotas (the rocky cove area) into town along a well-kept esplanade. Sapphire-blue Med on one side, pretty villas set in gardens full of pine trees on the other. Up above is Mount Montgo with its curious rocky outcrops.

Urbanizations (suburbs) ribbon out for seven miles along Les Marines, the sandy beach side of Denia. The ones nearer town are the pick of the bunch...the furthest urbanizations don't look overly desirable. Many apartment blocks were built in the late 1960s...and some desperately need a facelift. Prices are across the board, but the following samples will give you an idea of what your dollars will buy.

- Denia town—750-square-foot apartment with castle and port views, $70,800.
- Pego (inland village around seven miles from Denia)—village house to restore, $78,000.
- Denia—840-square-foot apartment in residence with communal gardens and pool, 300 yards from the beach, $147,700.
- Denia, Las Marinas—645-square-foot ground-floor apartment in a pretty residence with communal pool, 50 yards from the beach and 4.5 miles from Denia town, $156,000.
- Las Rotas, Denia—1075-square-foot apartment with 450-square-foot terrace in residence with pool, $187,000.
- Els Poblets, Las Marinas, Denia—terraced bungalow (1,030 square feet) in garden of 4,300 square feet, $242,800.

Crammed with picturesque corners, Altea (population 13,500)

rejoices in its title of the Costa Blanca's prettiest seaside village. Its landmark feature is its blue-domed church above an old town center of tangled alleys. Sugar-cube houses climb the steep hilltop, adorned with wrought-iron balconies and ceramic motifs of saints upon the walls.

A ground-floor, two-bedroom apartment (1,205 square feet) is being sold fully furnished close to Altea town. In a residence with communal pool, the price is $203,000. On La Sella development near Altea, a new villa (1,400 square feet) with large terrace and carport has views over a golf course and Mount Montgo. On a 3,200-square-foot plot, it's $348,000.

Dutch and Scandinavians are very keen on Altea—there's even a Norwegian school. What's probably saved it from suffering the same mass development as Benidorm—almost hidden behind the Sierra Helada—is the lack of sand. Beaches here are pebbly, but it has a really nice feel. A couple of miles from Altea town, one of the Costa Blanca's swishest developments is Altea Hills. The developers have their own website: *www.alteahills.com*. The cheapest property currently listed is a two-bedroom apartment overlooking the marina for $149,000.

Divided into three areas—old town, port, and El Arenal beach area—Javea (population 23,300) is very popular with the expat community. Fifty-one percent of the residents are foreign. Starting price for Javea is around $79,000. That buys a sixth-floor, one-bedroom apartment with elevator, private parking, and views of the sea and Mount Montgo.

Javea's old town is very pretty. Here a completely refurbished two-bedroom townhouse with roof terrace could be yours for $176,000. Unfortunately, the new settlement behind the port isn't overly attractive and already seems to be suffering from overdevelopment. Guarded by a line of ancient watchtowers, the hills above are also scarred with thousands of villas. It's not easy on the eye from down below.

A shame, because Javea has a spectacular natural setting. Hunkering between the cliffs of Cabo de San Antonio and Cabo de la Nao, it enjoys a warmer and dryer microclimate than other coastal locations. La Nao is also called "the Dawn of Spain" because this is the country's nearest point to the rising sun. Behind is Mount Montgo with a hairpin road corkscrewing across the hills to Denia.

Further from the town of Javea, things get better—though you will pay at least $360,000 for small secluded villas with lookouts over secret coves. Desirable areas include Cap Marti, El Tosalet, and El Balcon al Mar near La Nao. At Balcon al Mar, a 1,180-square-foot villa in a garden of 10,000 square feet with garage and pool is $378,000. At a Cumbre del Sol urbanization between Javea and Moraira, a terraced duplex (925 square feet) with established front garden, sea views, and communal pool is $163,000.

Now for Benidorm. This is definitely not Romantic Spain. Benidorm is the Spain of Union Jack shorts, warm beer, and all-day English breakfasts. The Costa Blanca's holiday capital, it probably won't be your idea of Spanish bliss. That said, it has thousands of fans—and 55% of visitors are repeat visitors. For many Britons, summer just wouldn't seem the same without a trip to "Benny."

Almost dwarfing the mountain setting, the skyline resembles Miami Beach...but the beaches are superb...if you can find space to try them out. As it's so popular, it's not particularly cheap for property. The 880-square-foot apartments in town are priced at $173,000. A five-minutes drive from the center, new 1,450-square-foot bungalows list at $201,000.

- **Mary Domus Inmobiliaria** (Catherine Sleiman), *Calle Calderon 10-B, 03700 Denia (Alicante); tel. (34)96-643-23-61; fax (34)96-642-60-56; e-mail: marydomus@marydomus.com; website: www. marydomus.com.*

- **World Class Homes** (Lisa Townsend), *Avda Lepanto 6-Bajo, 03726 Benitachell (Alicante); tel. (34)96-688-5280; fax (34)96-649-4068; e-mail: benitachellwch@telefonica.net; website: www.world classhomes.uk.* This company also has offices in Altea, Javea, Denia, and Moraira.

The Orange Blossom Coast

Travel an hour north of Valencia and you're in the heart of the Costa del Alhazar—the Orange Blossom Coast. Still largely untargeted by foreign vacationers and home buyers, it boasts acres of orange and almond groves as well as sandy beaches like those of the Costa Blanca. And it must be said that it shares some of the same high-rise developments...though that doesn't deter hordes of summertime vacationers from Madrid and other large Spanish cities.

With a population of just 12,000, Benicassim feels totally Spanish. Five wonderful sandy beaches stretch for almost five miles. And although there are some unattractive tower blocks, the backdrop of green mountains is unscarred by ribbon developments of bungalows. Criss-crossed with ancient pilgrim paths, these sierras are especially lovely at sunset when they take on a rosy pink glow.

Up until the 1930s, Benicassim was a fashionable place for Spanish society to spend the summer. A mile's walk from Benicassim town, the wide seafront promenade is lined with palm trees and turn-of-last-century villas. They rarely come up for sale but you could buy a 1,290-square-foot bungalow with large terrace in a development with communal pool for $262,000.

In the Oliva-Gandia area, Costa Azahar Homes is listing an 860-square-foot ground-floor apartment in need of some modernization for $72,000. It has two bedrooms, one bathroom, kitchen, lounge/dining room, and patio. A 645-square-foot apartment on the first line of Oliva beach is $96,320. A small country house in Miramar—ready to move into—is $93,600. It has three bedrooms, a bathroom, lounge, kitchen, and small garden.

- **Costa Azahar Homes,** *Calle Guillem de Castro, 8 bajo, Oliva 46780, Valencia; tel. (34)962-839-741; e-mail: info@costaazahar-oliva.com; website: www.costaazahar-oliva.com.*

Rental properties

For long-term rentals, you usually need a deposit the equivalent of one or two month's rent, and letters from an employer or bank showing proof of your ability to pay. If you use an agent, their commission is normally one month's rent.

Madrid excepted, rents for a two-bedroom apartment in a city can be $600 to $720 per month, while a three-bedroom house can be around $1,500 per month.

But, like along Portugal's Algarve, many rental properties on the Costas serve as holiday lets rather than catering for people seeking a long-term stay. That said, you shouldn't find it too difficult to get a long-term winter let. On the Costa de la Luz, Agencia Luz Atlantic has a number of attractive two-bedroom apartments and three-bedroom bungalows for $540 monthly over the winter. With sea views and close to bars and restaurants, one is right on the seafront promenade at Barrosa la Mar.

That's not to say long-term rentals don't exist on the Costas, but leasing in a vacation area on a full-year basis means you could be paying something like $1,225 monthly. That's the normal rental for a two-bedroom furnished apartment (750 square feet) in Barrosa la Mar.

A good website for finding non-vacation rentals is *www.tucasa.com*. Although the site is in Spanish, it's easy to figure out and the rents seem far lower than those through agencies that target the English-speaking market. In Jerez de la Frontera, an Andalucian town famous for its sherry bodegas, a one-bedroom *apartment totalmente amueblado y equipado* (fully furnished and equipped) is listed for $396 monthly. Near Cádiz, a two-bedroom, fully furnished apartment with private terrace in a small development with communal pool and garden is $649 monthly.

- Benalmadena (Costa del Sol)—one-bedroom apartment in residence with pool, $720 per month.
- Barcelona—670-square-foot apartment, $720 to $960 per month.
- Torrevieja (Costa Blanca)—two-bedroom villa with pool, $910 per month.
- Puerto Banus (Costa del Sol)—two-bedroom apartment, $960 per month.
- Madrid—430-square-foot apartment in the historical Los Austrias neighborhood, a five-minute walk from the Royal Palace, $1,320 per month.

- Madrid—1,450-square-foot apartment in residence with pool, crèche, near university, $1,800 per month.

When renting property in Spain—long or short-term—it's advisable to have a written contract. Tenants may be required to pay property tax and community fees if the contract so specifies. You should receive a receipt for all rental payments. Long-term tenants must take out third-party insurance for a property they are leasing.

What potential buyers should know

Away from the popular Costas, English isn't as widely spoken as you might expect. Realtors will happily give you listings, but with rock-solid local interest, they can afford to ignore the language skills needed to attract international clients. Further complicating matters, most people in Catalonia use Catalan rather than standard Spanish. Signs don't point to *la playa* (the beach). Here it's *la platja*. Milky coffee isn't *café con leche,* it's *café amb llet.* And a street isn't a *calle*—it's a *carrer.* The same applies to the Basque Country on Spain's northern Atlantic coast where many people speak Basque.

To get the most out of Spain, you'll probably need to make some changes to your lifestyle. Outside of the big cities, shops close for three-hour afternoon siestas, and restaurants rarely cater for early eaters. In fact, Spaniards don't usually have lunch until 2 p.m. or dinner before 9.30 p.m.

There's a nasty little thing about import duties. Household goods are duty-free if you're moving to Spain permanently, but if it's a second residence, non-EU citizens are subject to 12% duty on the value of the goods.

Buying your home

Once a property has been chosen, the first step is to make a verbal offer. You may wish to make this offer conditional to being able to obtain a mortgage. In a typical transaction for resale property, you put down an initial deposit ($3,600 to $7,200) to reserve a property. Ideally, e-mail or fax the reservation contract to your lawyer to check before signing. This initial deposit is refundable if the vendors change their mind, but without a clause like "subject to mortgage approval," you'll lose your deposit if you cancel because you can't get a loan.

A lawyer ensures that Spanish legal requirements are met and that the property is bought free of encumbrances, charges, liens, or debt. In Spain, any outstanding debts are transferred with the property—you obviously don't want to inherit someone else's back taxes.

You then sign a preliminary contract, the *compraventa,* and pay a portion of the purchase price, normally 10%. This is a legally binding contract that states the date of completion. At that time, all the parties —or their designated representatives—go to the *notario's* office to sign the *escritura,* the deed of sale. At that point you pay the balance of the purchase price along with all fees and taxes. Conveyancing normally takes around eight weeks.

As a general rule, you should allow 10% to 11% of the price of a property to cover associated purchase costs. Depending on how much work is involved, legal fees are between 0.5% and 2% of the purchase. Notary fees are fixed by law and normally range from $360 for lower-priced properties to $1,450 for higher-priced properties. Land Registry fees are generally about $360.

Then there's value-added tax (IVA) or transfer tax (ITP). ITP applies to resale properties only; IVA is levied on off-plan properties. Both are currently at 7%. Stamp duty of 1% is payable when purchasing off-plan.

Plus Valia is a local municipal tax based on the officially assessed increase in the value of the land since the last time the property changed hands. This tax is normally payable by the vendor, but it may be stipulated that the buyer pays. It can range from a few hundred dollars to as much as several thousand dollars on larger properties with a lot of land.

Fees and charges on purchases of real estate in Spain

Example based on a resale property costing $144,240:

- Spanish transfer tax (ITP) of 7%—$10,095.
- Stamp duty of 0.5%—$720.
- Notary fees—$600.

- Land registry fees—usually in the region of $360.
- Spanish lawyer—$1,440.
- Total—$13,219

Cost of ownership

Owners of Spanish property have to pay annual property taxes. They are based on *cadastral value*—the official value of your house for tax purposes—rather than the price at which it actually changes hands. Even in a region such as Andalucia, the tax can vary widely from town to town for similar types of property. As a rule of thumb, however, you can expect to pay around 0.2% of the cadastral value of your home.

You will undoubtedly pay more in property taxes for a townhouse in Puerto Banus than perhaps for a villa inland. If you decide to live in a typical village away from the coast, your annual real estate tax could be less than $80. On the other hand, if you live in a large villa with a private garden close to the sea, you could be levied as much as $2,200. For most apartment owners, property taxes are in the region of $250 annually.

Can you run a home for as little as $800 a year? Possibly...but at that level it's likely to be a village house or a very small apartment with little in the way of communal facilities.

Taking into account water, electricity, and upkeep charges, running costs of a typical two-bedroom apartment in southern Spain are in the region of $2,160 to $3,000 per annum.

Annual running costs for the average-priced three-bedroom villa or bungalow in a classy development are more likely to be somewhere between $3,500 and $4,500. This will also include water, gas, electricity, local rates, community fees, and house and contents insurance.

On the Costas, each development has its own annual charge for community fees that are set by the owners' association. This charge often covers water usage, refuse collection, and maintenance of the estate (public lighting, upkeep of common areas, security, etc.). The fee usually corresponds to the size of your plot or property as a proportion of the whole development.

A two-bedroom apartment or small urbanization home usually falls into the $720 to $960 price band in popular resort developments on the Costa del Sol; around $500 to $600 on the Costa Blanca. However, it can be as low as $250. Service charges for apartments in provincial cities aren't likely to break the bank either. For example, a refurbished 1,400-square-foot apartment in Cádiz old town priced at $295,800 has annual service charges of $518.

Electricity costs 10 cents per unit. You'll pay approximately $450 to $550 per annum for a two-bedroom apartment. Bills are only likely to be really heavy in the winter months (December to late February.) However, if you have air conditioning and give it a frequent workout, the cost will be higher. (Air conditioning costs upward of $1,350 to install.)

A 12.5 kilo bottle of gas for cooking costs $9.60. Your first bottle will cost around $35, which consists of a $25 deposit and a charge for the gas. From then on, you exchange an empty bottle for a full one and pay the normal rate.

Water is sometimes included in community charges, otherwise expect to pay around $90 to $330 per annum depending on where you live. Water is metered and charges vary from an average of around 85 cents per cubic meter on the mainland to $2.30 to $3.60 per cubic meter in the Canaries and some parts of the Balearic Islands.

Telephone installation costs $180; annual line rental is $200. Local calls cost around 10 cents per minute with a three-minute call to the U.S. coming in at around $1.30. Several ISPs provide free Internet service, though the local call to the provider still carries a charge. Connection speeds are 40 to 48K. Broadband costs around $55 per month.

Running costs for a Spanish townhouse

Here are the running costs of a 1,600-square-foot townhouse in a complex with pool and gardens in Calahonda on the Costa del Sol. Priced at $309,600, it has three bedrooms, two bathrooms, a newly equipped kitchen, lounge (with fireplace, terrace, and garden), and satellite TV. It is close to all amenities.

- Community fees (includes water)—$160 a month or $1,945 a year
- Local rates and property taxes—$575 a year
- Electricity and gas—$770 a year
- Telephone-line rental—$200 a year
- Insurance—$250 a year
- Total—$3,740 a year

Cost of living

Living costs in Spain are fairly low, even in the cities. Leaving aside rent or mortgage payments—and depending on your lifestyle—a couple could easily live on $11,000 to $12,000 and still eat out regularly.

Once you know where to go, a meal for two with wine can cost as little as $20. For the best value, choose the lunchtime *menu del dia* (the menu of the day). Although the food is likely to be more filling than fancy, there's normally a choice of dishes on the three-course lunchtime menu. In most places, the *menu del dia* usually costs between $7.50 and $10.

A local beer and a tapa (a little snack which can be anything from a couple of rings of fried squid to a slice of ham topped with an olive) costs around $1.40. Even dining in classier restaurants isn't overly costly. For a couple, the bill is usually somewhere between $45 and $70 —wine included.

Obviously grocery bills are hard to estimate, but the typical spend per person is $70 weekly. You can go to the cinema for $5.40 and get a mid-range seat in the shade at Madrid's bullfighting arena for $3.80 ($3.50 for a seat high up in the sun.)

Unlike 25 years ago, there is no shortage of good hospitals and private clinics along the southern Costas. However, costs for private health insurance vary enormously—though you're likely to find it far less expensive than at home. Comprehensive policies for people 55 to 60 years old go from $860 annually up to $2,000. A routine visit to a private doctor is normally $35 to $55; home visits are from around $50 to $110, depending on whether it's day or night. The cost of a bed in a private hospital is in the region of $135 per day. Include doctor fees and you can reckon on about $275 per day for the duration of any stay.

State health care is considered good and available for free or at reduced costs. However, you must be contributing to Spanish Social Security or be receiving a state pension from another EU country to benefit.

Paying your taxes

Under Spanish law, all non-residents with assets in Spain are required to appoint a fiscal representative to carry out their tax duties. Foreign residents in Spain must file an income tax return for personal obligations and worldwide income. Income tax rates go from 18% to 48% on earnings above 67,435 euro ($80,900). If you reside more than six months per year in Spain, you are considered a tax resident even if you have not obtained a residence permit.

Certain types of income (like public pensions for complete and permanent invalidity) are exempt from income tax. There are also double taxation agreements between Spain and a number of countries including the U.S. If you have already paid income tax abroad, you can deduct this from your Spanish tax bill.

Spain has an annual wealth tax—the *patrimonio*. It's levied on assets in Spain: property, bank accounts, cars, bonds, stocks, and shares. Non-residents are subject to wealth tax only on assets in Spain, whereas residents also pay taxes on offshore assets.

For residents, the wealth tax only applies to property worth over $180,000. For non-residents, the tax is levied on all property, no matter what the value. It can be based on either cadastral value, purchase value, or the value estimated by the tax authorities—whatever is greater. The wealth tax is set at 0.2% for assets up to $197,000, and goes up to a maximum of 2.5%.

When you decide to sell

Over-65s are exempt from capital gains tax on the sale of their home if it's their primary residence. Otherwise residents are taxed at 20%; non-residents at 35%. To ensure the tax is paid, Spanish law requires that you pay 5% of the total purchase price directly to the tax agency if you're a non-resident. So, only 95% of the selling price goes into the vendor's bank account. If the tax turns out to be less than this deposit, the balance can be reclaimed.

Chapter 8

Switzerland

Picture a sun-drenched, white house with a shady courtyard, Switzerland...Who hasn't dreamed of living in a cozy Alpine chalet or an elegant apartment overlooking a mirror-calm lake? The attractions of high living standards, low crime, and fantastic infrastructure aren't to be sneezed at either.

Switzerland is a highly desirable place to live (particularly for the well-heeled). The Swiss currency has been one of the most attractive in the world for international companies and wealthy individuals.

In addition, taxes in Switzerland are low for those who earn their fees in the international marketplace, and the country has excellent financial centers through which to deploy investments. And almost everybody must have heard of "numbered bank accounts" which offer secrecy and anonymity.

Despite what you may think, Switzerland isn't just for the mega-rich. Although there are restrictions about where and what you can buy, you don't have to be a resident to own a Swiss home. And not all properties cost $1 million or more. In mountainous French-speaking Switzerland, around the Villars-sur-Ollon area, bijou studio apartments sell for just over $100,000. A three-bedroom chalet in Gryon could be yours for $284,000. Built way back in 1733, this postcard-pretty chalet is 1,600 square feet.

At home in Switzerland

Switzerland's immigration laws are tough. With only seven million citizens, the Swiss are determined to preserve their identity. A bilateral agreement with the EU means restrictions aren't quite so rigid for EU nationals, but for others it's difficult to get a foothold. You'll find it difficult to obtain a permit allowing you to settle permanently in

Switzerland, since there are immigration quotas. If you are over 60, don't intend to work, have some ties with Switzerland, and assets of over CHF 1 million ($790,000), you may stand a chance.

That's not to say you cannot buy a vacation home in certain parts of Switzerland. Providing the local commune of a canton gives authorization, you are allowed to own one apartment or chalet with up to 200 square meters of habitable space (2,150 square feet). You can rent it out as a holiday let—and also live there yourself for three months at a time. Most non-EU nationals can stay up to six months in any one year.

But...these are only the general federal rules. Switzerland is divided into 26 cantons, and each has its own laws. The majority of cantons completely restrict the sale of second homes to foreigners. Buying in cities such as Geneva, Lausanne, Basle, Berne, Zug, and Zurich is completely prohibited.

Depending on whether there's a glut of foreigners purchasing property, the rules on where you can buy vacation homes are apt to change every year. For the moment, the largest choice of properties for sale is in French-speaking Switzerland—in Vaud, Valais, and Jura cantons. In Vaud canton, you can buy in Montreux, Vevey, and some other Lac Leman lakeside towns. The mountain resorts of Villars-sur-Ollon (Vaud canton) and Verbier (Valais canton) are also open to non-Swiss buyers. A one-bedroom apartment of 400 square feet with balcony in Verbier costs around $190,000.

You can also buy in parts of German-speaking Switzerland, but properties tend to be higher priced—and restrictions are usually stringent in the extreme. In affluent Klosters, only three or four newly built properties are authorized for sale to foreigners each year. In Grindelwald, foreigners are only permitted to buy chalets and apartments valued over $474,000 and $632,000 respectively. But don't bother thinking about Zermatt—you cannot buy there at all.

Lake Lugano in Italian-speaking Switzerland is also feasible. However, get in-depth advice. For a current update on cantonal rules and regulations, we recommend you contact Simon Malster of Investors in Property. This London company works with Swiss agents on the ground. According to Simon, purchase fees vary between cantons, but are never more than 5% of the acquisition price.

Western Switzerland

A wonderful place for summer (or winter) vacations, western Switzerland packs in some awesome splendor. In this region you are never far from lakes, mountains, or both. This is the French-speaking part of the country: *la Suisse*.

You'll quickly realize that German-speaking Switzerland doesn't have the monopoly on cowbells...needle-spired churches...or Alpine chalets brimming with window boxes of geraniums.

A skier's playground in winter, Villars-sur-Ollon in Vaud Canton is part of the Alpes Vaudoises and is linked to the glacier skiing at Les Diablerets. The surrounding area, which includes the villages of Gryon, Chesnieres, and Barboleuse, boasts 146 ski lifts serving over 70 miles of pistes. It's a charming village—very low-key—with alluring views of the jagged teeth of the *Dents du Midi* range. And...foreigners can buy holiday homes here without a residency permit.

At 4,265 feet up on a sunny shelf, and home to around 3,500 inhabitants, Villars-sur-Ollon has an impressive range of summer activities too...including a golf course. While it costs around $537,000 for a new 1,100-square-foot chalet in Villars itself, you could buy a centrally located apartment (450 square feet) for $130,000. And Gryon (3,655 feet up) turns up cheaper options. A five-bedroom chalet is $418,000; one-bedroom apartments of 480 square feet sell for $95,000.

Unlike some ski resorts, Villars is tailored for families, not party animals. If you aim to rent your holiday home during the ski season, the most lettable properties are two-bedroom apartments in central Villars or Barboleuse. Properties of 700 to 750 square feet average $250 to $285 weekly.

The Swiss Riviera

Lac Leman (often wrongly called Lake Geneva) is tagged "the Swiss

Riviera." Summers are definitely Riviera-like: in July 2003, the mercury hit 95° F. Relatively speaking, winters can be quite mild, which explains the terraced vineyards. In fact, it's mild enough for palm trees to flourish in Montreux.

Deep blue-green, dotted with sailboats, Lac Leman suggests Swan Lake come to life. It's spellbinding to watch these graceful birds, especially the swans that patrol the looking-glass waters under medieval Chillon Castle. In summer, numerous ferries ply between the lakeside villages and the elegant cities of Geneva and Lausanne. Ferries also go to Evian (source of the famous bottled water) in France.

Vladimir Nabokov, Charlie Chaplin, Noel Coward, and Freddie Mercury—all owned homes in Montreux and neighboring Vevey. Ambling the Quai des Fleurs, a lakeside promenade between these neighboring towns, it's easy to understand why. You'd never tire of the panorama of lakes, Alpine pinnacles, and twinkling villages. And within a half-hour, you can be high in the mountains. It's fabulous in spring when the upper meadows become a blooming mass of narcissi.

Foreigners don't need a residency permit to buy a vacation home in Montreux, Vevey, and a number of other lakeside towns. However, unlike in the mountains, prices are fairly high. In general, you can estimate around $350 to $490 per square foot.

Montreux is a Belle Epoque town whose grand hotels wouldn't look out of place on the French Riviera. A 1,100-square-foot apartment with views of the lake and Savoy Alps costs $387,000. Vevey has enormous cachet too. On its *bord du lac esplanade,* a 1,020-square-foot apartment with two balconies is $498,000. On the edge of Vevey's old town—also with lake and mountain views—a 2,060-square-foot apartment is $948,000.

Christiane of Montreux's CGS Immobiliere says foreigners can also buy holiday homes in the lakeside settlements of Chexbres, Clarens, and La Tour-de-Peilz. More affordable, but you'll still pay $47,000 to $71,000 for small studios of 290 to 325 square feet in Clarens. In Montreux's Terrinet suburb, a 560-square-foot apartment is $217,000.

The Bernese Oberland

Each commune in the canton of Berne (German-speaking) sets its own rules for foreigners. One place to consider is Wengen. High above the Lauterbrunnen valley, the village has some of the most dramatic views of the Alps. It's a charming and rather old-fashioned resort...though the Old World feel can probably be put down to the fact that the village is traffic-free. You can only reach Wengen by a cog railway built over 100 years ago.

Though it's almost impossible for foreigners to buy chalets within the village itself, you could buy in the near vicinity. Twenty minutes from Wengen, a three-bedroom chalet is priced at $316,000. No problem with buying apartments: two-bedroom units mainly fall into the $213,000 to $455,000 range.

Grindelwald is "the glacier village"—the largest and oldest resort in the Jungfrau region. The peaks of the Eiger and Jungfrau tower above and spill their glaciers almost into the village itself. Here foreigners are only allowed to buy apartments having a market value of more than $474,000 and chalets over $632,000.

Lake Lugano

La Dolce Vita, Swiss style! Clinging to the southern edge of the Alps, Lake Lugano belongs to the Italian-speaking part of Switzerland. The climate is more Mediterranean than Alpine and residents enjoy plenty of sunshine.

One of the Switzerland's most popular holiday resorts, the town of Lugano has a beautiful lakeside promenade. Towering up above are the mountains of Monte San Salvatore and Monte Bré. There are some appealing villages both in the hills and on the lakeshore: Morcote, Melide, and Gandria.

While foreigners can buy a vacation property in Lugano town and a number of villages, prices are substantially higher than across the border in Italy. A 730-square-foot apartment with small terrace and views of the lake lists for $387,000. A larger apartment (1,030 square feet with terrace of 205 square feet) in a residence with shared pool is

$636,000. As for a classic 2,150-square-foot chalet with its own pool in the hamlet of Vico Morcote, prepare to dig very deep indeed: $1,343,000.

Real estate agencies for Switzerland

- **Investors in Property,** *120 West Heath Road, London NW3 7TU; tel. (44)20-8905-5511; e-mail: sales@swissproperty.com; website: www.swissproperty.com.*

- **Gerance Service Le Muveran,** *Case postale 90, CH-1884 Villars-sur-Ollon; tel. (41)24-495-35-35; e-mail: office@gerance-service.ch; website: www.gerance-service.ch.*

- **CGS Immobilier,** *Grand-Rue 98, CH-1820 Montreux; tel. (41)21-962-70-50; e-mail: g.stam@cgs-immobilier.ch; website:www.cgs-immobilier.ch.*

Renting in Switzerland

If you are here on a work assignment through a company, or you have a residency permit, typical rents for furnished, long-term properties are:

- Studios—$550 to $990 a month.
- One-bedroom apartments—$790 to $1,425.
- Two-bedroom apartments—$1,225 to $1,950.
- Three-bedroom apartments—$1,560 to $2,870.
- Four-bedroom apartments—$2,200 to $4,635.
- Four-bedroom townhouses—$3,750 to $6,600.

Restrictions and obtaining a permit to buy

Non-residents can buy vacation homes in certain areas. Only properties in a few of the cantons are authorized for sale, and they're usually in resorts with tourist attractions. EU citizens who are Swiss residents can buy without restriction. Other residents can buy one property for their own use. You also have to seek special permission if you want to buy a plot of land larger than 3,000 square meters.

Throughout the whole of Switzerland, the annual quota of permits made available to foreigners wishing to purchase property currently stands at 1,440. As well as limiting the geographical area in which foreigners are permitted to buy, Swiss law also restricts you to buying certain types of property. In some cantons you can buy an individual chalet, in others you cannot.

There may also be restrictions relating to the resale of property. In some cantons foreigners are prohibited from selling property within five years of purchase. In others they may sell immediately. The time it takes to obtain a permit to buy also varies from canton to canton. Generally, getting one in the Canton of Vaud (which includes the mountain resort of Villars and the lake resort of Montreux) is the easiest. Permits there are usually approved in two to three months.

Residency permits

According to the Swiss Embassy, "Foreigners who do not wish to engage in a gainful activity (work) and do not intend to study in Switzerland may stay for a period of up to three months without a residence permit. Visitors who travel to Switzerland on a regular basis, but stay for less than a three-month period each time, must apply for a permit if their total stay exceeds six months within a 12-month period."

Without huge amounts of wealth at your disposal, residency permits are very difficult to obtain. You must be over 60, retired, and show some close links with Switzerland.

- **Embassy of Switzerland,** *2900 Cathedral Ave. NW, Washington, D.C. 20008; tel. (202)745-7900; website www.eda.admin.ch/ washington-emb.*

Buying your home

Different cantons...different rules and procedures. However, in most cantons, after you have agreed on terms with the seller or their agent, and obtained your permit to buy (or residence permit if applicable), you make an appointment with a local public notary. This is a sworn officer of the court whose responsibility it is to ensure the transaction is legal. The notary acts for both the purchaser and the vendor. A notary checks that the vendor owns what is being sold, and that you have the right to buy it. The money is paid to the notary and released only when the change of ownership has been properly registered.

Regarding purchase fees and taxes, these are usually payable by the buyer directly to the public notary. The amount varies from canton to canton but is generally around 4%. In canton Valais (Verbier) the total purchase costs—notary fees, land registry fees, and government purchase taxes—amount to around 2.5% of the purchase price. In canton Vaud (Villars) the total costs are 5% of the purchase price. The property must be purchased in the name of a private individual; it is not permitted to buy in the name of a limited company. Real estate agents also normally charge a commission of around 1%.

As Swiss inheritance laws will apply, it is advisable to make a will that refers specifically to the property, and to lodge a copy with the notary.

Obtaining finance

Depending on status, Swiss banks will generally lend up to 65% of the purchase price over 25 to 50 years. A Swiss mortgage is secured against the property and can be fairly flexible. The borrower pays interest every six months on the capital outstanding and can pay off part of the loan on giving notice. Interest rates are currently around 4.5%.

Cost of ownership

Property taxes vary from canton to canton and are usually between 0.8% and 1.2% of a property's value. Service charges can add another 1%. For an apartment in Verbier you should estimate approximately $6 per square foot for taxes and charges—utilities, insurance, communal charges, and local property taxes.

In Vaud canton, which includes the mountain resort of Villars, taxes, charges, and utilities amount to around $9.50 per square foot. The lake resort of Montreux is a little higher, but bills shouldn't amount to more than $7,000 annually for the upkeep of a small apartment.

Even with service charges, annual payments shouldn't be more than 2.2% of the property's value.

Sample housing costs in Switzerland

- Electricity for domestic use is charged at 20 cents per kWh plus 7.6% VAT.

- Natural gas is charged at 8 cents per kWh plus 7.6% VAT.

- Telephone rental is $20 per month; the local call rate is 7 cents a minute during the day.

- Annual household insurance premiums start at $105 per $40,000 of cover.

You may want to offset the costs by renting your property out as a vacation let. Rental agencies usually charge around 20% commission for providing a full rental and management service. Most owners rent their apartments through such agencies on a weekly basis, and set aside a week or two each season for their own use. Rental income is not taxable in Switzerland, but it may be taxable in your country of residence.

Cost of living

With an average after-tax income of around $48,000 per year, Swiss residents are among the world's wealthiest citizens. Even humble cleaners get hourly rates of around $15 to $20.

For eating out, many brasseries and restaurants offer a lunchtime *plat du jour* (dish of the day) for $9.50 to $13.50. However, in the evening it's *a la carte* and you're talking serious money, even in brasseries. One main dish: $30. Dessert: $7. A bottle of wine—another $30.

It takes determined foraging to even find pizzas for under $12. The average price for a coffee is $2.60...for a small beer, $3.80. By small, I mean 33 cl—three mouthfuls and it's gone. If you're not financially reckless, stick to *vin ouvert* (open wine) served by the glass or carafe instead of a bottle of wine. A half-liter carafe of wine usually goes for around $12. Tap water is safe, so drink it to cut costs. Bottled water can be as much as $4.75 per half-liter in some establishments.

When you decide to sell

Switzerland does not levy capital gains tax, except for professional equity and real estate traders.

Paying Swiss taxes

Apart from saying that most Swiss citizens pay income tax of around 30% on their income, the Swiss tax regime is far too complicated a subject to cover here: each canton and even city may have different tax rates. There are opportunities to negotiate a lump-sum fiscal tax deal with the authorities. If you think you may be eligible for a permanent resident permit (and remember, there are quotas), you should seek the advice of a tax specialist.

Chapter 9

The Eastern Front:

Europe's Emerging Markets

All property is theft? Don't know about that, but not too far back, the ownership of property in the former Eastern Bloc countries was illegal. There was no chance of a local having a stake in the housing market, let alone a foreigner.

Now things couldn't be more different. And with a number of new countries becoming full EU members in 2004, the appetite of foreign investors for eastern European properties shows no sign of slowing. Prices have boomed, but values still remain substantially lower than in Western Europe—and so do living costs.

While Eastern Europe will never be ranked as a classic sunshine destination, summers are a lot warmer than you might imagine. (And besides, not everybody is a sun worshipper.) The Czech Republic, Hungary, and Poland are definitely interesting places to consider if you're looking for a home in more unusual "foreign parts."

And, as well as having a fantastic experience, you may make a good profit from your investment. But...while the potential for rewards may be great, there are more risks involved with buying in Eastern Europe than in countries with a longer history of home ownership. Take legal advice, and make sure title is absolutely watertight before making any financial commitment.

Czeching out the Czechs

Why consider the Czech Republic? High living standards, low living costs, and the prospect of good gains on real estate with EU membership. Since the 1989 Velvet Revolution, the Czech Republic has rapidly approached Western living standards. However, costs are substantially lower than in the country's western neighbors, Germany and Austria. According to Czech Invest, average prices in Prague are only 43% of those in Vienna.

Invariably spotlessly clean and litter-free, some Czech towns are in the regeneration stage. Although back streets often show grimy evidence of decades of neglect, staggering attempts have been made to restore places to their former glory.

Tourists rediscovered its capital, Prague, in the years following the Velvet Revolution. The city was compared to Paris in the 1920s—cheap and arty, with its history, culture, and architecture. Prices rose, of course, as the world's writers, artists, tourists, and investors came in greater numbers. But few ventured outside the capital, and, even today, the Czech countryside remains completely undiscovered.

Prague the Golden

Prague the Golden, the City of a Hundred Spires—what Goethe called the "prettiest gem in the stone crown of the world." No doubt about it, Prague (*Praha* to its citizens) is one of Europe's most wonderfully atmospheric cities.

Home to 1.1 million people, the Czech Republic's capital has always been a magnet to writers and painters, artists, and intellectuals. Architectural ecstasy awaits at every turn. The Old Town is a bedazzlement of gilded statuary, Gothic spires, pastel-colored houses with russet roofs, and baroque palaces adorned with cherubs. Cross the Vltava River over Charles Bridge—lined with watchtowers and ornate statues turned to blackened stone—and you're in the equally historic Castle district.

The only somber note in this city of delights comes from Death, ringing out the hour on the astronomical clock on Prague's Old Town Hall. This is the cue for the mechanical figures of saints to start their famous hourly parade.

Property has become fairly expensive in Prague, certainly compared to other parts of the Czech Republic. However, in relation to other

European capitals, it offers good value. Prices mostly range from around $140 to $235 per square foot, though it does shoot higher in the Prague 1 district.

First though, it needs stressing that buying isn't as straightforward as in Western countries. At present, foreigners need to set up a company to purchase Czech real estate—both in Prague and elsewhere. This doesn't require huge amounts of capital—it's normally $6,000 to $7,000.

Still a relatively small city, Prague is now officially divided into 15 districts. Rather confusingly for would-be home buyers, most real estate agencies stick to the old district numbers of 1 to 10.

Prague 1 is the oldest part of the city. On either side of the Vltava river, it takes in the Castle and the Charles Bridge. As most historical sights are located here, it's an obvious choice for investors as well as expat singles or couples without children. Along with the Old Town Square, Malá strana, and the Jewish Quarter, this is also where you'll find Wenceslas Square and Na Poíkopi, a pedestrian area of hotels, casinos, restaurants, and shops.

Renovated apartments in restored buildings can fetch over $280 per square foot, but there are still good deals going for less. Through Reality 21, $189,600 buys a 1,140-square-foot apartment close to Wenceslas Square. They also have a third-floor, two-bedroom, 750-square-foot apartment for $161,000.

In Prague 1, monthly rents of $2,000 to $2,200 per month are being sought for many two-bedroom apartments of around 1,075 square feet. However, with many locals on wages of under $500 a month, these rents are unaffordable to all but the highest-paid Czechs. Most furnished apartments for short-term vacation rental are also located in Prague 1.

Professionals agency has a good selection of long-term rentals in most parts of the city. Within the old center itself, they have a newly refurbished, one-bedroom apartment for $2,240 per month. At almost 1,200 square feet, it's quite large by old center standards and the rent includes the cost of a night security guard. Again, though, you can still find reasonable rents if you hunt around. Listed in the real estate section of the *www.prague.tv* site, a 645-square-foot furnished apartment is $765 monthly.

Prague 2 and 6 are also good districts to buy into, and there's a diverse selection of property. Second on the district-desirability scale comes Prague 2, a residential neighborhood of early 20th century apartment houses. Through Reality 21, a 430-square-foot apartment in a three-storey brick house with garden is $71,800. Prague 6 is also considered to be an address with cachet. Home to a large number of embassies, Prague 6 is also handy for kids who go to the International School of Prague.

Prague 4, south of the center, is a large district that includes hypermarkets, agricultural land, and good residential areas.

On the castle side of the Vltava River is Prague 5. Shrewd investors are starting to look at this area. The northern part contains new residential and commercial developments—many new shopping centers are located here. The southern end is full of industrial remnants from Prague's past, though the area is undergoing a transformation. Many of the old Baroque and Art Nouveau properties are being cleaned up and restored.

In Prague 5, near the Vltava River and still fairly close to the old center, Tide Reality has a 1,070-square-foot apartment on the 4th floor of a building. Priced at $243,000, it has two bedrooms and was recently modernized—there's a fully fitted kitchen and hardwood floors throughout.

At Smichov, also in Prague 5, Air Reality has a "superior" apartment for rent, part of a restored Art Nouveau villa with garden. A terrace can be accessed from either the living room or the bedroom. With a large bathroom and fully fitted kitchen, it rents at $560 per month.

If you want more space or need a place for a family, far better value can be had away from the old center. Other things to bear in mind are proximity to schools, public transport, and parking.

One Prague 5 property that meets all of those conditions is offered through Reality 21. In a quiet residential area, this two-storey family house (5,500 square feet) stands in its own garden. It's a five-minute walk to Jinonice metro station. The house was built in 1931, has three bedrooms, a ground-floor verandah and is described as in good condition. Asking price is $190,400.

The same agency has a nice property in the desirable Prague 6 district. With a view over Hvezda Park, this three-bedroom house is on two floors and in good condition. Total floor space is 3,800 square feet with a garage of similar size. The property also has a small outside office that was converted from a garage. The price tag of $306,200 reflects the area's standing.

IL subscriber Carolyn Carr owns and operates Property News, a property search and information service in Prague. She says investors who confine their searches to Prague 1 and 2 are often disappointed. Foreign investors have placed so much demand on a limited supply that property prices in those areas have already increased dramatically. She feels that the potential for yields going forward may be low and buying into these sought-after districts has to be regarded as a longer-term investment.

Few investors would consider sinking money into the Prague world of panelaky—the high-rise, Soviet-style apartment blocks made of concrete panels. These still house most of the city's population, but many buildings are now in a perilous state.

Prague realtors and agencies

- **Property News** (Carolyn Carr), *Pod Parukarkou 6, 130 00 Praha 3; tel. (420)271-771-717; e-mail: propertynews@czech-realty.com; website: www.propertynews.cz.*

- **Reality 21 s.r.o.**, *Starochodovska 1359, Praha 4; tel. (420)271-122-123; fax (420)267-910-921; e-mail: reality@reality21.cz ; website: http://www.reality21.cz/.*

- **Tide Reality s.r.o.**, *Svobodova 9, Praha 2; tel. (420)224-920-152; fax (420)224-920-680; e-mail: info@tide.cz; website: http://www. tide.cz.*

- **Professionals s.r.o.**, *V. Celnici 4/1031, Praha 1; tel. (420)224-934-680; fax (420)224-934-982; e-mail: info@professionals.cz; website: http://www.professionals.cz/.*

- **Air Reality,** *Borivojova 54, Praha 3; tel. (420)222-719-134; fax (420)222-717-235; e-mail: air-reality@iol.cz; website: http://www.air-reality.cz/.*

Once you've bought or rented a property, Prague is a cheap place to live. The average monthly wage is still little more $400. Even on the tourist trail you can get a half-liter of lager in an old-style beer cellar for $1.30 and a plate of roast pork, dumplings, and red cabbage for $3.50. Off the beaten track, prices are even cheaper—a plate of goulash and a glass of beer is $2.

Prague citizens spend an average $50 to $100 monthly on utility bills, while real estate tax works out to around $50 per year. Elsewhere in the Czech Republic, utility costs are likely to be even lower.

A Bohemian lifestyle?

The Czech Republic divides into the regions of Bohemia and Moravia. Blessed with hot summers and Christmas-card winters, Bohemia is a spellbinding mosaic of romantic castles and towns straight from sword-and-sorcery tales.

Frescoed houses and Rapunzel-style turrets are fairly common throughout Central Europe—and Bohemia has its share. But have you ever peered into a medieval bear-pit complete with bears? Seen a chandelier made entirely from human bones? Or cricked your neck staring at a *stoupa*...a lofty "Plague Pillar" adorned with saintly statues and chained devils? These *stoupas* commemorate deliverance from the plagues which swept Europe during the Middle Ages.

The countryside is studded with wildflower meadows...dense forests of silver birch and spruce...and ponds full of fat, lazy carp. You'll also see fields planted with hops, enough to meet the Czech thirst for beer—the biggest in the world. A vital ingredient in the brewing process, hops have been cultivated here since the 9th century. King

Wenceslas (of Christmas carol fame) recognized their importance: those caught exporting hop cuttings got sentenced to death.

Bohemia's property market

Cottages to restore start at less than $5,000. Some are admittedly ramshackle, but you can find homes in excellent condition at reasonable prices. RIS Agency has an exceptional bargain at a village called Sedlec, near the old silver-mining town of Kutna Hora. Just 50 miles from Prague, this cottage is 850 square feet and was built 10 years ago. Priced at $47,000, it has three bedrooms and over 6,000 square feet of garden.

Depending on area, land ranges from 15 cents to $5.70 per square foot. If you want to build a new house, properties of 1,650 square feet generally cost between $61,000 and $92,500 including the plot.

You'll also see smart-looking wooden houses for between $15,000 and $25,000. However, tempting prices don't always tell the whole story. That Sedlec cottage would make a permanent home, but not all properties are suitable for year-round living. Wooden summerhouses (alternatively known as recreation houses) often look well-cared for, but they can be basic. While many are placed handily near local ski resorts, few people would want to live in a summerhouse in January when temperatures plummet below freezing.

Sometimes buried deep in the forests, recreation houses usually have no heating, electricity, or indoor toilet facilities. They're probably best for back-to-nature types. Water is obtained from spring wells, lighting from kerosene lamps, and appliances such as refrigerators (if you have them) only work on bottled gas. Even so, $24,000 seems reasonable for a three-bedroom wooden chalet on 3,500 square feet of land in a forest location 30 miles from Prague.

Karlovy Vary—a star spa

80 miles west of Prague, Western Bohemia has some exceptionally picturesque spa resorts. The best known are Karlovy Vary and Marianske Lazne. These may be more familiar to you under their old Germanic names of Karlsbad and Marienbad.

For centuries, Bohemia's therapeutic spas hosted the cream of European society. Peter the Great of Russia, Edward VII of England, and the Empress Maria Theresa of Austria...Beethoven, Chopin, and Liszt...Schiller, Turgenev, and Gogol...Goethe who created a scandal with his affair with a 16-year-old wench. The renowned German writer was 72, so obviously there's something to be said for the waters.

The fame of Karlovy Vary, the grandest of Bohemia's spa towns, dates from the 14th century. Legend has it that a Bohemian king called Charles the Fourth discovered its healing springs while hunting, when an injured hound fell into a stream and its leg was instantly cured.

Built along the Tepla River, the town maintains an aristocratic air. Rising in tiers toward wooded uplands, Baroque and Art Nouveau mansions are painted in delicate sugarplum shades. Elegant colonnades are topped with statuary; parks blaze with rhododendrons and azaleas; shops sparkle with crystal, Bohemian garnets, and glassware beaming with bejeweled color.

There's an almost Swiss sense of cleanliness. No litter, no graffiti, and the only blot in the sylvan setting is the Hotel Thermal, built in Czech communist times. A funicular wheezes up through the woods to the Diana Tower, a Gothic lookout. This is the starting point for a network of forest walks patrolled by red kites and other birds of prey. Opportunities abound for long hikes as the trails meander for 60 miles. They're well-maintained too—workers actually sweep leaves off the woodland trails.

Karlovy Vary real estate averaged a 10% rise last year. The most desirable area is the spa quarter where refurbished apartments can fetch over $230 per square foot. Capitol Reality has a 2,650-square-foot home with six bedrooms and sauna for $610,000. At the other end of the scale, a 600-square-foot unmodernized unit is $69,000. Improvement costs (nobody wants old-style gas heating systems any more) are estimated at $12,500. The Architecta agency has a similar-sized apartment near the Colonnades for $54,000. But you get twice as much space in the business district. Here, a 1,500-square-foot modernized apartment in a turn-of-last-century building lists at $104,000.

With Russian investors uninterested in the rural lifestyle, cottages in Karlovy Vary's countryside haven't seen the same price hikes. They start at $14,000. In the small village of Zlutice, a five-roomed, two-storey house is on offer (through Recom Reality) for $14,200. The house, built in 1851, has two bedrooms and floor space of 2,300 square feet. On a 4,600-square-foot plot, it was reconstructed in 1991.

Beer Heaven—Ceske Budejovice

South Bohemia's largest settlement—and a regional capital—Ceske Budejovice (pronounced Chesky Budiyov-ITZY) has 100,000 inhabitants. Its old name was Budiwoyz. The city became known as Budweis during the years that the country belonged to the Austro-Hungarian Empire. Until 1945, half the city's population was of German stock. The local beer (*pivo* in Czech) was thus called Budweiser beer. Its brewing history goes back six centuries. Despite what you may think, Budweiser isn't an original U.S. product.

Half-liter glasses brimming with golden Bud cost 45 to 55 cents. And at 10% or 11% proof, it's feistier than the beer sold in the U.S. One place to sample it (along with goulash and dumplings) is in a cavernous beer hall called Masne Kramy, the town's arcaded main square featuring a fountain of Samson. From medieval times until the 19th century, this church-like building housed the town's meat market. Patrons sit inside chapel-like areas (they were the former butcher shops) on either side of a central aisle.

One local realtor with buys in the nearby countryside is Pavel Crha of Hornik Agency, whose pretty wooden summerhouses in these parts start at $14,400. In a village called Cichtice, $23,500 also seems reasonable for a small stone-built cottage suitable for a couple. Although it only has an attic bedroom, it has electricity and water and you could live here year-round. The ground floor consists of a kitchen, living room, and bathroom.

Within Ceske Budejovice itself, Hornik's has a large two-storey row house for $61,000. The ground floor consists of four rooms previously used for a small business. The second floor has three bedrooms, kitchen, and bathroom.

South Bohemia's lakelands

A 30-minute drive from Ceske Budojovice takes you to Trebon's lake district. In medieval times, villagers set up a complex of fishponds to raise carp—a freshwater fish that's still the mainstay of Christmas Eve dinner tables. South Bohemia once had 5,000 of these fishponds.

Founded in the 13th century, Trebon is a toytown of 9,000 people which you enter by one of three arched gates. Vestiges of ancient bastion walls remain...track them and you'll come across a house that once belonged to the local hangman. It also has an ornate main square with old-fashioned inns, a Plague Pillar, and a Renaissance-style chateau with an immaculately kept park. On spring afternoons, the benches are taken up with grannies busy with wool and knitting needles.

Properties through Josef Kolar of Trebonska Realitni Kancelar include a two-bedroom house in Trebon for $68,000. Just three miles into the countryside, a large farmstead with a good quality, three-bedroom house costs $93,000. With 230,000 square feet of land, the property would make an ideal recreational or business opportunity for equestrian lovers. One of the four outbuildings already has three stables in place.

All woods, meadows, and lakes, the area around Trebon has a number of marked forest walks. This is prime bird-watching territory with cormorant and heron colonies on the pine-covered islands. The complex of fishponds also attracts waders, grebes, goldeneye ducks, and white-tailed eagles. And if you tire of birds and fishponds, there are plenty more castles and fortresses to discover. Between the 12th and 16th centuries, the inhabitants of southern Bohemia built 500.

Cesky Krumlov

Many towns and cities describe themselves as medieval—which usually means they have a medieval quarter. In Cesky Krumlov, the Middle Ages completely swallows you up. A storybook town of 15,000 inhabitants near the Austrian border, it was added to UNESCO's World Heritage List in 1992.

Almost untouched by time, Cesky Krumlov is divided by the fast-flowing Vltava River. On one side of the river is Latran neighborhood, dominated by a fortress-like castle looking down on a huddle of red-roofed gingerbread houses. Clamber towards the castle and you'll come across a bear-pit...with three bears. It's an old tradition dating back to the 1500s.

From Latran, wooden bridges lead to the core of the old town with its 14th century frescoed houses. Cobbled streets wind towards a main square complete with a Plague Pillar. Cesky Krumlov's *stoupa* was built to give thanks for delivering citizens from the plague of 1680 to 1682.

Most properties in the historic center are now businesses. This means prices are high—a 1,800-square-foot house renovated in 1995 was $355,000. Better value lies in the leafy suburbs. Currently divided into two apartments, an attractive two-storey yellow house (2,000 square feet) is $187,000 through Renom Reality.

Hornik Agency has a 300-year-old stone house for $9,200 in nearby Horice na Sumave village. Ripe for reconstruction (but not tumbling down), it's a row house with two downstairs rooms, a basement, and garret. There's a sewage connection, new electricity line, and the garden is 6,000 square feet.

Silver and bones in Kutna Hora

In 1400, King Wenceslas moved his royal court to Kutna Hora in Central Bohemia. Forty-five miles from Prague, this quaint town has 22,000 inhabitants. The silver mines brought incredible wealth and its proceeds went to the creation of some magnificent buildings: palaces...cloisters...a Plague Pillar...the huge Cathedral of St. Barbara, patron saint of miners.

If you love places full of stories, you'll adore Kutna Hora. Along the back roads—in summer smothered in white elderflowers—is a lane called Ruthardska. This was named after Rozina Ruthard, a medieval wild child. Her father certainly didn't believe in free love, but she did, so he walled her up in a closet and she smothered to death.

We don't know if Rozina got buried in Sedlec, but don't miss this place. Now part of Kutna Hora's suburbs, Sedlec has one of the most gruesome sights imaginable—an ossuary (a bone house or bone chapel). Thousands of skulls and bones are displayed, but not all in quiet repose. The chapel contains chalices, heraldic symbols, and even a chandelier—all made from human bones.

In 1278, a local abbot visited Jerusalem, returning with earth from Golgotha which he sprinkled on Sedlec graveyard. Not surprisingly, everybody then demanded to be buried here. Space got even tighter when the Plague of 1318 wiped out an estimated 30,000 souls in this small region alone. The brainwave of a half-blind monk, the ossuary was built in 1511. Bones were formerly piled in heaps, but in 1870 a Czech prince donated 12,000 gold coins to turn the chapel into a macabre work of art.

Kutna Hora is thoroughly engaging. However, while many buildings have been restored, a good number remain dilapidated. Sadly, some 15th-century houses seem too far gone. Their frescoes have completely faded and the stonework is crumbling to dust.

RIS Agency has properties in town, but the least expensive renovated home is just over $140,000. Rental apartments of between 700 and 1,200 square feet cost $210 to $370 monthly. The small villages surrounding Kutna Hora offer plentiful bargains. A two-storey house in Albrechtice u Malesova is $78,500. Built in 1959, the house is in good condition and comes with over 97,000 square feet of land.

Bohemian realtors

- **Recom Reality s.r.o**, *Varsavská 13, 36001 Karlovy Vary; tel. (420) 353-228-545; fax (420)353-228-546; e-mail: recom@recomreality.cz; website: www.recomreality.cz.*

- **Architecta Realitni, T.G.** (Miroslav Ptak), *Masaryka 42, 36001 Karlovy Vary; tel. (420)608-224450; e-mail: ing.ptak@volny.cz.*

- **Hornik SRO** (Pavel Crha), *Novohradska 1, 37001 Ceske Budejovice; tel./ fax (420)38-6357787; e-mail: hornik@hornik.cz; website www.hornik.cz.*

- **Trebonska Realitni** (Josef Kolar), *Husova 69, 37901 Trebon; tel./ fax (420)333-723-861; e-mail: trebonrk@treb.cz.*

- **Renom Reality** (Rene Mracek), *Namesti Svornosti 7, 38101 Cesky Krumlov; tel./fax (420)380-711-640; e-mail: info@renom.cz.*

- **RIS Agentura** (Michaela Spackova), *Vocelova 342, 28401 Kutna Hora; tel. (420)327-511-243; fax (420)327-511-937; e-mail: office@ ris-kh.cz; website: www.ris-kh.cz.*

Purchasing Czech real estate

At present, there are restrictions on buying real estate by foreigners in the Czech Republic. Real estate may only be bought by permanent residents or by officially registered "legal entities."

Foreigners normally acquire property by establishing a limited liability company. The capital required is approximately $6,000. The realtors listed above can help you form a company and find a Czech partner (required for the first three months). This partner is in name only, and you control all company assets. The next step is to inform the Czech Embassy that you own a company and require a working visa. This qualifies you to obtain a long-term residency visa, renewable annually.

- **Embassy of the Czech Republic,** *3900 Spring of Freedom Street, NW, Washington, D.C. 20008; tel. (202)274-9103; fax (202) 363-6308.*

Real estate transfer tax is 5% plus around $20 to record change of ownership in the Land Register. Be aware that the buyer becomes the lawful owner of a property only after a record has been made in the Land Register. Conveyancing may take up to several months. To minimize the danger of fraud, the bank normally acts as a guarantor by issuing an irrevocable letter of credit. Alternatively, a public notary receives the money from the buyer under secure conditions and hands it to the seller only after the record in the Land Register has been certified. Both banks and notaries are officially authorized by the government to provide such services.

Paying your taxes

Czech residents pay income tax on worldwide income. Non-residents pay income tax on Czech-source income only. Residency is defined by having a permanent home in the Czech Republic and/or residing in the Czech Republic for at least 183 days in any consecutive 12-month period. Tax rates are progressive up to the top rate of 32%.

All companies and individuals are subject to property tax, but it's very low, rarely more than $50 annually for homeowners. It's calculated according to the ground area of the building. It's 4 cents per square foot for business premises and less for residential buildings.

Hungary

Hungary...the gaily colored butterfly that emerged from the gray chrysalis of communism. Not quite Western Europe, but not quite Eastern Europe either, it sits snugly at the heart of what the Germans call Mittel Europa and we sometimes call Central Europe.

Budapest is the focus of most foreign investors, but consider looking outside the capital. The Hungarian countryside is mostly unspoiled: a tapestry of lakes, wooded hills, cornfields, vineyards, and acres of nodding sunflowers. Sure, winters can be pretty bleak, but summers are bathed in lazy, golden splendor...and temperatures can hit the 90s.

Budapest—two cities in one

The Hungarian capital is actually two cities in one. Until medieval times, Buda and Pest were separate settlements. Still touched with Mittel Europa's prewar sparkle, both sides of the city are adorned with lovely Baroque buildings from the glory days of the Austro-Hungarian empire.

Budapest is an exhilarating place to consider living. Home to 2.5 million inhabitants, it's vibrant, bustling...a city madly in love with the new, but reluctant to bid farewell to its past. A sizeable expat community is already in the capital as this is the preferred headquarters for corporate Central Europe. Although detached houses are often expensive, small apartments of around 635 square feet in renovated buildings go for under $70,000 in many good neighborhoods. Nice rentals start at $420 monthly.

An investment opportunity? Well, the ideal time to have bought was three or four years ago. In the best neighborhoods, prices have risen by 100% in the last two years. Over four years they've tripled. Some Hungarians have made small fortunes. When housing was "privatized" in the late 1980s, sitting tenants had the "right to buy" and could avail of up to 85% discounts against market value.

That said, prices in the affluent areas of Pest (Districts 5 and 6) remain reasonable by the standards of western European capitals. You can find two-bedroom renovated apartments of around 1,000 square feet from $98,000 to $123,000.

There may still be lots of mileage in Budapest property, but do take advice from a variety of sources—more if you are buying for investment. Maintenance standards have been poor: around half of all city apartments are in need of renovation.

Buda Hills

Hilly Buda is the capital's oldest part. This is District 1, site of the Fisherman's Bastion, pattering fountains, ornate churches, quaint houses, carved statues, and much else besides. Beyond this "Castle Quarter" is Budapest's most desirable residential area, District 2, a place of leafy avenues and individually built townhouses and villas nestling below wooded hills.

Prices of detached properties in District 2 (on Buda's side of the Danube) have rocketed over the last eight years. There are a few areas in this district, often referred to as "the Beverly Hills of Budapest" that are a popular choice with Hungary's rich and powerful. Prices here can seem high in comparison to similar properties in other districts.

Piramis agency has a bungalow-style house in the area for $ 247,000. With 1,215 square feet of living area, the house would be perfect for a couple. Built in 1950 and in very good condition, it has good views over the surrounding hills, a small terrace, and large garden.

Eurocenter Real Estate Agency has a large selection of quality properties in some of Budapest's best neighborhoods, including District 2. For example, a six-bedroom, 8,100-square-foot house with a large garden goes for $1,491,000. Luxury does not come cheap but for that price you get an indoor swimming pool, large sauna, three bathrooms (each with a Jacuzzi), and a garage that accommodates several cars.

That's a bit of an exception. In general you can expect to pay between $430,000 and $920,000 for new and refurbished individual villas (2,700 to 5,500 square feet) in the prime Buda Hills districts 2, 11, and 12. Prices are about 15% to 20% lower for comparable quality in Districts 2A and 3, which are further out from the city center.

District 12 is another very prestigious address. Perhaps the most exclusive neighborhood in Budapest, it's home to Hungary's president and prime minister, numerous ambassadors, and an increasing number of Hungarian celebrities. Villas rarely come on the market, and when they do, expect to pay a minimum of $1.8 million.

Prices for new apartments in the premier Buda Hills Districts 2 and 12 range from $230 to $400 per square foot. Much depends on the location of the residence, the quality of interior finishes, and the level of amenities such as on-site fitness club, pool, and concierge.

Rents in District 12 also vary widely. A three-bedroom ground-floor apartment in a villa is available through Eurocenter for $1,580 per month. The same agency has an attractive four-bedroom, three-bathroom semi-detached house for $2,700 monthly.

Apartment picks in Pest

The commercial heart of the capital, Pest, is flat—a place of wide boulevards and pavement cafés. However, it's no 21st century metropolis. Buildings have a *fin de siècle* feel. You come across all kinds of lavish curiosities: mosaic-tiled roofs flashing in bejeweled colors, gilded turrets and cupolas, and bathhouses resembling fairytale palaces. One of the most elegant boulevards is *Andrassy ut,* particularly the stretch near City Park where there's a zoo whose animal houses could have been designed by a Far Eastern potentate.

One of the highlights of Budapest is its mineral spa baths. *Szechenyi Furdo* are outdoor baths right in the City Park—an ideal place to relax after tramping around realtors' offices. While the sugarplum yellow and cream spa buildings are grand, it only costs $3.70 for a two-hour ticket. Unlike the more famous Gellert baths that draw the tourists, it's mostly Hungarians who visit Szechenyi's medicinal waters—and even soak over games of chess. These thermal pools are open even in winter: in one, the water is heated to 94° F.

Pest is an apartment city, and the most sought-after districts are 5 and 6. In general, square-foot prices in these neighborhoods go from around $105 to $205, depending on the need for refurbishment, the size of the apartment, and the quality and condition of the building itself. Many residences are in the grand 19th-century style, built around inner courtyards that are invisible from the street. Those that have been renovated are lovely: high ceilings, wooden floors, and often embellished with ornate carvings and other period features. Here are some examples from Casaro Hungary Ltd.'s portfolio:

- In downtown Budapest, on Fovam utca (*utca* means street), in District 5, the banking area. With a view of the garden courtyard, this two-room apartment (815 square feet) is on the third floor of a riverside building. Price: $112,000.

- On Eotvos utca in District 6, a second-floor apartment of 1,105 square feet with courtyard view. This four-room apartment is in a building (one of only four in the city) designed by Alfred Eiffel, of Eiffel Tower fame. The apartments are being sold prior to restoration work due to commence in 2004. Price: $128,300.

- On Saint Istvan Street in District 13, close to the Comedy Theater. This four-room apartment of 1,545 square feet is centrally located and only in need of minor renovations. The building itself was only recently restored. Price: $167,700.

District 7, a rather run-down area of Pest, has thus far been neglected. This may represent an opportunity for the intrepid as most apartments are currently valued at between $40 and $65 per square foot. However, it's unlikely that you'd want to live in one yourself at the moment. According to a report in *Budapest Business Journal,* 30% of apartments here are "comfortless"—lacking basic amenities such as bathrooms or inside toilets. And there's no huge glut available: many are rented as social housing.

If you don't shudder at the phrase "five-year-plan," there's talk of District 7 getting a major facelift, walkways, and a pedestrian zone. Private property developers are already foraging. Once sitting tenants have been relocated to other neighborhoods, it's possible the values of new-build apartments will match those in classier districts. Some already seem to. Casaro is offering a 1,150-square-foot, top-floor, two-bedroom apartment on Dohany Street for $170,500.

It may also be worthwhile taking a look at some outlying districts. Although District 14 is the third-largest and second-greenest in Budapest, it has had to wait for regeneration. A former industrial area, it is now quickly improving. Modern apartments are being constructed in green surroundings—prices start at around $125 a square foot.

District 22, on the Buda side of the Danube, is often referred to as the "town of champagne and wine." Hungary's major champagne and wine companies operate from here. Though primarily urban, the district does include areas of industrialization and Communist-era "panel" high-rises. The area is just beginning to develop its potential for wine culture tourism. And demand for houses in the green areas is boosting values. Kala & Eppel Real Estate is offering a 3,200-square-foot, seven-room detached house in the elite Rózsavölgy area for $396,000. The property is in excellent condition and comes with a 7,650-square-foot garden and two-bay garage.

Budapest rentals

A number of agencies in the rental market target expatriates. Most of their long-term rental properties are priced in U.S. dollars or euros. Apartments are very affordable, but houses in the best areas are expensive: from $3,000 to $7,000 monthly for detached properties. The following are offered through Casaro and Eurocenter:

- District 6 (Pest): Cozy, renovated apartment (515 square feet) with a courtyard view on a very good location on Terez krt. Fully equipped, modernized kitchen, washing machine, DVD-player, cable TV. $420 monthly.

- District 5 (Pest): Suitable for a single tenant, a 535-square-foot apartment, totally furnished with antiques. In the city center, it has one bedroom, living room, bathroom, and kitchen. In a renovated, old-fashioned building, shops and restaurants are on the doorstep. $492 monthly.

- District 2 (Buda): Newly refurbished furnished apartment (645 square feet) with a view of the Parliament. $600 monthly.

- District 2 (Buda): Furnished with IKEA-style furniture, a two-bedroom, two-bathroom villa apartment (965 square feet) in green surroundings. $660 monthly.

- District 5 (Pest): Beautifully renovated and furnished apartment (1,260 square feet) in a prestigious location, close to Andrassy street. Fully equipped and modernized kitchen (refrigerator, microwave, oven, dishwasher), cable TV, VCR, alarm system. $1,080 monthly.

Budapest realtors

- **Casaro Hungary Ltd.**, *1051 Budapest, Sas u, 4; tel. (36)1-486-3500; e-mail: info@casaro-hungary.com; website www. casaro-hungary.com.*

- **Kala & Eppel Real Estate**, *1015 Budapest, Csalogány u. 6-10; tel. (36)1-212-4756; e-mail: realestate@kala.hu; website www.kala.hu.*

- **Eurocenter Real Estate Agency**, *Varosmajor ut 50b, H-1122 Budapest; tel./fax (36)1-212-9050; e-mail: info@eurocenter.hu.*

- **Piramis Real Estate Agency**, *Verecke ut 8, 1025 Budapest; tel./fax (36)1-33-55-965; e-mail: piramis@mail.datanet.hu.*

- **HungarInvest Ingatlan Bt,** *Falk Miksa u. 12. I.em. H-1055 Budapest; tel. (36)1-373-0513; e-mail: info@hungarinvest.com; website: www.hungarinvest.com.*

Into the Magyar heartlands

Away from Budapest, you'll find a world where winsome village houses and rural properties often sell for between $15,000 and $45,000. They're habitable, all have basic facilities, and they're not buried in the wilderness—most are an easy drive from some really attractive towns.

Take this one at Mezokovesd, a two-bedroom detached house built in the 1970s. Modernized and in good condition, the property is 900 square feet on a 5,700-square-foot plot. Price: $44,000. A small town of around 18,000 inhabitants, Mezokovesd is the focal point for the Matyo, a Magyar people noted for their folk art and fine embroidery. From here its only 11 miles to Eger, a strikingly colorful town that's full of historic gems including some beautiful Baroque churches and a 16th century minaret dating from the days when Hungary was ruled by the Turks of the Ottoman Empire.

Home to 62,000 inhabitants, Eger is just under two hours by train from Budapest. It's famous for *Egri Bikaver*—Bulls' Blood—one of Hungary's most popular red wines. Behind the bull's head motif on labels lies a curious story. In 1552, Eger's townsfolk were besieged by Turkish invaders. When not engaged in battle, the menfolk fuelled themselves with gallons of local wine—staining their beards red in the process. Glimpsing what appeared to be blood-covered beards, the Turkish camp became rife with rumors that Eger's ferocious defenders undoubtedly got their strength from supping the blood of bulls...

The place to sample this mythical brew is in *Szepasszony-völgy,* which loosely translates as "The Valley of the Nice Woman." ("The Nice Woman" was apparently a lady who used to keep a bawdy house in the valley.) A 30-minute stroll from the center of Eger, it has dozens of little wine cellars run by families with vineyards in the area. Kind of like a French *cave,* most cellars have tables and chairs inside where you can sit and try before you buy. A liter costs less than $2.

In the Eger region, close to the small village of Mezonagymihaly, is a solid "farmers cottage" for $27,000—which shows that some properties are as great a value as the wine. With good access to the motorway, this three-bedroom house sits on a 16,000-square-foot plot. The sale price includes a stable and old farm outbuildings. The Bükk mountains provide a backdrop for most small towns and villages in this area. Craggy limestone hills rather than mountains, they get their name from the numerous beech trees growing in the region.

Something cheaper? Well, $13,500 buys a ready-to-move-into, centrally heated three-room cottage with kitchen and bathroom near a hamlet called Mezokeresztes. Fifteen miles from Eger, the house was built in 1940 and renovated in 2000. The cottage sits on a 26,000-square-foot plot.

It's actually possible to buy for even less than that. Numerous properties in the area are described as "ideal holiday or weekend homes." However, like Czech summerhouses these kind of properties usually lack even the most basic comforts. No electricity, no water—and no bathroom or toilet. They're totally unsuitable for habitation during a Hungarian winter.

- **Bukkalja Estate Agency** (Eva Toth Bencze), *Gesztenye utca 26, 3400 Mezőkövesd; tel. (36)20-9770-531; e-mail: webmaster@ hungaromax.com; website: www.hungaromax.com/ingatlan/english.html.*

Sprechen Sie Deutsch?

Rural tranquillity, bargain-priced homes...you may wonder why you hear so little about the Hungarian provinces. Yet some foreigners *are* buying here—quite a few homes are owned by non-Hungarians: Germans, Austrians, and emigrés with Hungarian ancestry. Why so few others have bought is undoubtedly down to one major hitch: language difficulties.

Outside of Budapest, tracking down English-speaking realtors is quite literally like looking for a needle in a haystack. If you were serious about searching for provincial property, the wisest move would be to employ an interpreter and translator. The properties listed above are on offer through one of the few agencies that can do business in English.

Are most Germans and Austrians linguistic wizards? Of course not, but it's an easy market for them to negotiate as realtors can usually converse in German. Buyers from German-speaking countries are specifically targeted. You'll come across a number of agencies that are German-owned. They don't call themselves by the Hungarian title for realtor *(Ingatlan)*, but *Immobilien*, the German word.

For those who don't want to employ an interpreter on any initial house-hunting foray, the language situation isn't entirely hopeless around the Lake Balaton area. After all, most Germans speak English too...

Lake Balaton

Sixty-seven miles southwest of Budapest, Lake Balaton is land-locked Hungary's main holiday region. Almost 50 miles long and 12 miles wide, this is Europe's largest lake outside of Scandinavia. It's just like being at the beach...the silty bottom of the lake feels just like sand. You can wade out for almost a mile before the water comes above your knees.

Dozens of little resorts and villages string its shores—most going by the name of Balaton-this or Balaton-that, and there are plenty more settlements in the wine-growing hinterland on both sides of the lake. Basically, the further removed a village is from the lake, the cheaper properties are likely to be. That doesn't mean having to go miles away: within a 15-mile radius you can find simple peasant cottages for $14,000 and restored farmhouses (with bathrooms) for $56,000 to $70,000.

Tagged "Hungary's Summer Capital," Balaton's largest community is Siofok, on the southern shore. In the summertime, numerous ferries putter across the lake from here to various villages.

Around 23,000 people live within Siofok municipality, and it has the biggest choice of banks, restaurants, and supermarkets...plus a pretty park with a fishpond, Victorian-style bandstand, and a white-spired church.

However, you may get the feeling that you've arrived at Deutsch-land-on-Sea. During high summer, it gets as many German vacationers as Hungarians. Cafés have signs saying *echte deutsche Kaffee* (real German coffee), most market goods are priced in both forints and euros, and postcards carry greetings from the *Plattensee*, the German name for Lake Balaton.

Siofok has some imposing villa-style houses, though the nearer they are to Lake Balaton, the more the prices hot up. Even so, they're a fraction of what homes are selling for in Budapest. The sum of $240,000 buys a 2,115-square-foot villa with a turret. Built in 1940, it sits in gardens of 5,820 square feet.

In Balatonaliga village, five miles out of Siofok and 400 yards from the lake, a cottage with a pretty flower-filled garden is offered for $112,000. Built in 1990, and with all necessary facilities, it's 1,675 square feet in size on a plot of 10,000 square feet. Procent Agency also has an "off plan" development of apartments close to the shore of the lake. Ranging in size from 600 square feet to 1,020 square feet, prices go from $99,000 to $144,000.

Laced with thermal springs, Balaton's northern shoreline is more picturesque because of the hilly backdrop, but the water can be reedy and the bathing not quite as good as on the south side. Balatonfüred's Immobilienmarkt has around 500 cottages and farmhouses on their books. Refurbished cottages near the lake start at around $46,000, but prices drop if you head for the hills...and plenty of restored farmhouses are available for under $50,000.

At the western end of the lake, Fonyód has become one of the most popular resorts on Lake Balaton. An attractive settlement of about 5,000 people, it has several thermal baths in the vicinity. There is even a geothermal lake—locals say that you can see steam rising even on the coldest winter's day. The Plattensee Süd Real estate agency has a wide range of properties both in the town and surrounding villages. In the countryside, eight miles from Fonyód, a 7,500-square-foot, fully renovated thatched cottage is $36,500. In a tree-filled plot of over 11,000 square feet, the cottage has two bedrooms, living room, kitchen, and bathroom.

In town, the agency has a family house 300 yards from the lake for $92,000. Built in 1990, the two-storey detached house stands in a

10,000-square-foot garden and has three bedrooms, two bathrooms, and almost 2,200 square feet of living space. Similar properties fetch $500 a week as vacation rentals during July and August.

Star buy has to be a pretty, pink-washed cottage just six miles from the thermal spa at Buzsak. For $19,000 you get a cottage—in good condition—with 750 square feet of living space. It has two bedrooms, living room, front room, kitchen, and bathroom and is on a 43,000-square-foot plot.

Lake Balaton realtors

- **Procent Immobilien** (Csaba Szabo), *Szechenyi ut 11, H-8600 Siofok; tel. (36)84-510-140; fax (36)84-510-142; e-mail: info@ procent.net; website: www.procent.arker.hu/site/index.htm.*

- **ImmobilienMarkt Balaton** (Istvan & Steffi Torma), *Helka ut 4, H-8230 Balatonfured; tel. (36)87-341-209; fax (36)87-481-615; e-mail: immobalaton@hu.inter.net; website: www.immobalaton.hu.*

- **Plattensee Süd Immobilien (Stephan Bors),** *Ady Str 5, H-8640 Fonyod; tel. (36)85- 363718; e-mail: plat-sued@mail.matav.hu; website: www.balaton.net/plattenseesud/index.asp.*

Buying Hungarian property—your options

Hungary's present socialist government reversed many of the policies of the former right-wing regime, which attempted to obstruct foreigners from buying residential properties in the capital. (There were few problems in buying elsewhere in Hungary.) Although in almost all instances where permission was refused and the courts eventually ruled in the buyer's favor, it was an unwelcome hassle.

Since 1996, foreign buyers have accounted for just under 8,000 apartments and houses in Budapest, less than 1% of the housing stock. (Although there's quite a bit of German activity around Lake Balaton, buyers from the English-speaking world rarely look beyond Budapest.) Recent changes have streamlined the approval procedure, but you should still engage the services of a lawyer to handle your transaction.

Investors planning on multiple purchases are usually advised to set up a local limited liability company.

To purchase property as a private individual, non-Hungarian citizens must apply for a permit from the local municipality (district council). A contract is signed and the money is then usually deposited in a lawyer's trust account. The contract should include a clause that allows the buyer to either cancel the contract if a permit is denied—or to transfer the contract to a company that will be established by the buyer. Purchase costs—notarial lawyer's fee, stamp duty, and agency fee will amount to around 9.5% to 10%. However, not all agencies charge a 2.5% to 3% fee to both the buyer and the seller. You may be able to shave costs down to 7%.

Many lawyers advise foreign nationals to set up a company registered in Hungary. Establishing a company will cost around $700 in legal fees. You must also deposit around $14,000 in a bank account until the company is registered. Annual fees for an accountant and auditor amount to $500 to $550.

Alternatively, you can buy an existing limited liability company off the shelf for around $600. The apartment is bought by the Hungarian company, which is wholly owned by the foreigner. One advantage of purchasing as a company is that while an individual pays around 6% purchase duty on an apartment, a company pays only 2%. When the company sells its properties, corporate tax is 18%.

Purchasing procedures

- The notarial lawyer (whose fees are charged to the purchaser, but represents both sides) will obtain the title deed (*Tulajdoni lap*) from the Land Registry office and check ownership. (Although Hungary does have a registry, not all properties are yet listed.) The notary will not countersign any contract of sale until it has been verified that the owner is really the owner and that there are no unsettled debts on the property.

- An agreement between the purchaser and the vendor about the price, conditions of payment, and the circumstances of taking possession will be drawn up. Allow one to two weeks for money to arrive from overseas by bank transfer. Foreign checks are not accepted in Hungary, and the down payment of 10% must be paid in cash.

- A further meeting between the seller, buyer, and notary is arranged. The contract must be signed in the presence of all parties and a representative of the real estate office.

- After signing the contract, the buyer must pay the purchase tax and notary and agency fees.

- The act of taking possession of the property is only carried out once the full price has been paid. The vendor declares receipt of the purchase price by signing a document. Taking possession happens at the property. Gas, electricity, and water meters are read, keys are handed over to the buyer along with statements from the utility companies that there are no debts on the property. The new owner is obliged to register utilities in his or her name.

Rental income and taxes

Whether buying as individuals or companies, most foreigners rent their apartments to non-Hungarian nationals who are working in multinationals and financial services companies in Budapest. Rental management companies typically charge a 10% rental fee, plus a 10% maintenance fee after the client has moved in. Investors can expect to get 7.5% to 10% of the value of the property in rental income, subject to local taxes of 20% to 30%.

Poland

A land of 9,000 lakes and vast open spaces, Poland is hemmed by the Baltic Sea to the north and the Carpathian Mountains to the south. Although largely pancake-flat, there's something soothing about its landscape. Tiny villages cluster around churches, head-scarved women hoe up onions, white storks flap toward untidy nests built atop telegraph poles. Deer often emerge from the mushroomy forests of silver birch and pine trees—the home of wild boar, brown bears, wolves, and wildcats.

Unless you're determined to trail around industrial splotches like the steel town of Nova Huta, Poland delivers up far more beauty than blight. Traveling through the countryside, you realize "the New Europe" is a misleading catch phrase. Rural Poland isn't Old Europe, it's Ancient Europe. It's an open picture book of little haystacks, horse-drawn plows, and meadows scythed by hand.

In May 2003, Poland voted "yes" in their referendum to join the EU in 2004. A jubilant President Aleksander Kwasniewski said the country was returning to "the great European family."

In theory, Poland should benefit from EU entry. And capitals always seem to benefit most of all. Warsaw's apartment market looks affordably tempting for investors—prices are pitched below those in Budapest and Prague. Most quality apartments in central Warsaw are fetching $115 to $140 per square foot.

But if you expect huge capital appreciation, we'd have to advise cautious optimism. Most analysts rate Hungary as having the best investment prospects in the eastern European region. Second comes the Czech Republic. Poland—the largest of the new EU members—is actually ranked third.

Although there's a shortage of affordable local housing in Warsaw, there's an oversupply of quality apartments—the kind of places expatriates rent for $1,500 to $2,000 a month. And if a new influx of corporate suits doesn't materialize, you'll not get rich by renting to the average Warsaw citizen. Take this 1,365-square-foot apartment in Zoliborz neighborhood. It's in a new low-rise building and has what the agents describe as a small "winter garden" with floor heating. On the market for $200,000, it's currently rented to a tenant who pays $320 monthly.

Like Warsaw property prices, rents have been in a rut for the past year. "There are a lot of people in the market and rents aren't as high as they used to be," said Darek Karbowniczak of Warsaw's Ober-Haus agency. "Prices should rise again, but it won't happen overnight. They will go up eventually, but it depends on income levels going up too."

The unemployment rate in Poland is 18%. The average monthly wage is just $635. And with one heck of a lot of office and retail space in Warsaw standing empty—estimates put it at 20%—it doesn't suggest the good times are rolling just yet.

Many Westerners who came to Warsaw as privatization specialists have now packed their bags and gone home. They have been replaced by locals whose salaries are far lower. This obviously affects the rental market.

Another point. Whereas a short-term Warsaw rental market could possibly develop through a new wave of EU bureaucrats seeking a home from home in the corridors of power, don't put any faith whatsoever in holiday makers. Tourists don't flock here, probably because there's not a great deal for them. Nearly 85% of Warsaw was obliterated by Nazi bombs during World War II. With its skyline of cranes and proliferation of "business plazas," there's no way it can be described as a must-see destination.

Warsaw's small medieval quarter has been rebuilt, but the city has few elegant 19th-century apartment houses similar to what you find in Budapest and Prague. Pre-war buildings don't exist and an "old" apartment is something from the 1950s. Diehard fans of Communist-era architecture can buy for under $50 per square foot.

Where Warsaw's expatriates rent

Needless to say, those expatriates still in Warsaw mostly prefer quiet green areas outside the city center—in suburbs where the views are less brutal, crime is less prevalent, and the air is cleaner. Studded with embassies and international schools, the leafy southern enclaves of Wilanow and Konstancin are the most desirable residential areas. In these neighborhoods, the average family home has living space of 2,700 to 5,000 square feet and rents for $4,000 to $5,000 per month.

The cheapest house currently listed in Konstancin is a 2,150-square-foot property for $170,000. The dearest, at $1.3 million, a "luxury family home (6,980 square feet) suitable for an ambassador or company chairman." Near the American School, a 4,835-square-foot house with four bedrooms and three bathrooms has a price tag of $450,000.

Wilanow is the site of the Wilanowski Palace, summer residence of Poland's former kings. There are duplexes here as well as houses—a 1,610-square-foot apartment in an attractive Mediterranean-style development with fitness club and sauna is $225,000. An apartment like this rents for $1,500 per month.

Kraków—a better prospect

Kraków, Poland's second city, may offer better investment potential. Reminiscent of Prague, this university city was once the royal capital and is a tourism showpiece. With a plethora of restaurants and good night life, it has plenty going for it as a short-break destination. Unlike most of Poland's cities, it escaped undamaged from WWII.

On average, quality apartments in the center of Kraków cost around $100 per square foot. There is already a thriving short-term rental market. One-bedroom apartments (430 to 915 square feet) are fetching $55 to $120 nightly; two-bedroom apartments (1,180 to 1,400 square feet) go for $90 to $120 nightly; and three-bedroom apartments (1,400 to 1,611 square feet) from $110 to $160.

And it's the tourist market you should aim for. While Kraków is Poland's premier university city, few students have rich daddies. A typical one-bedroom apartment in the center costs around $43,000, but you couldn't charge a long-term Polish tenant much rent. Even for quality properties of 540 to 645 square feet, the rent can sometimes be as low as $55 monthly. For properties of this size, you rarely see any monthly rent pitched higher than $320 for long-term tenants.

Location, location, location. Studio apartments list for as low as $25,000, but not on the right side of town. One studio is that price in Podgórze. We don't know if the current tenant is a student, but $25 a month rent isn't exactly a princely sum.

Steer clear of the suburb of Nova Huta. Although new-build apartments cost a mere $55 per square foot, you might have some difficulty persuading foreign visitors to stay here. Nova Huta was the site of the former Lenin Steelworks—and judging by the look of the place, those architects with a passion for Stalinist design haven't all gone away.

Fortunately, you don't need to spend ages mulling over where to buy in Kraków—not if you aim to attract the short-term rental market. Tourists are lazy creatures and want everything on their doorstep. So concentrate on the Old Town.

About $30,000 should get you a gem in a desirable area. For example, $36,700 buys a renovated 35-square-foot Old Town apartment near Plac Matejki. Moving up the price scale, $201,000 is the price of an Old Town apartment with 2,010 square feet of living space. Quiet and bright (there are large windows) it has connections for the Internet and cable TV in each room. It already operates as a short-term rental: $500 per week with cleaning service.

Though $134,000 for 710 square feet of living space is way over the notional Krakow average of $100 per square foot, you have to factor in the view. This apartment looks out onto the Vistula River and Wawel Castle. And if that isn't enough to tempt tourists, the Smocza Street address should prove an additional attraction. Smocza means "dragon." This street is only a step away from the Dragon's Cave, one of Kraków's highlights.

Here's one worth conceding: a 540-square-foot top-floor apartment in Kazimierz. It also has a view of Wawel Castle, but the cost is only $33,500.

Why the huge price difference? Well, it's not in the Old Town proper. Although the neighborhood is within walking distance of the Old Town, Kazimierz has only just begun the gentrification process. Until the Second World War, this was Krakow's Jewish neighborhood —scenes from *Schindler's List* were filmed here. But although the initial impression is of dismal gray streets, the neighborhood is on the up. New cafés, bars, and restaurants are appearing, apartment houses are being refurbished, and events such as the summertime Jewish Festival will help to pull in visitors. It may take a few years before Kazimierz rivals Kraków's Old Town, but the potential for property gains is huge.

What you can buy in Poland—and what you can't

The Poles don't make it easy to put money into their property market. Despite EU membership, stringent regulations continue to apply—even to citizens of other EU member states.

Without special authorization from the Ministry of Internal Affairs, foreigners can only buy apartments or plots up to 0.4 hectares (roughly an acre) in urban areas. A holiday cottage with a couple of acres? Not without permission—but as habitable 650-square-foot cottages with 10 acres in the Krakow countryside start at $11,000, you might attempt going through the red-tape.

Things ease up once you've been living in Poland for five years and have a residency card. However, even if you can stick it out for that long (think of those winters!), you'll still need special permission to buy in border areas such as the Tatra Mountains. This is where you'll find the country's biggest ski resort: Zakopane. Incidentally, although Zakopane is one of Poland's coldest places, it's actually the property market's hottest spot. Square-foot prices for new-build apartment properties are between $125 and $150. Not an overly attractive resort though. It's unlikely to tempt foreign skiers away from Europe's main resorts in France, Austria, Switzerland, or Italy.

Because of the unenviable history of foreign invasion, many locals fear the prospect of foreign investors gobbling up Poland's comparatively cheap land. With 20% of the population employed in the agricultural sector, Warsaw lobbied hard during EU entry negotiations for an 18-year transition period before foreigners could freely buy land. They didn't quite get what they wanted, but they got enough to make the EU's much vaunted "freedom of movement" charter look pathetic. Brussels agreed that without explicit government clearance, foreigners could be barred from buying land for 12 years after Poland joins the EU.

According to the Polish Embassy in Washington, the following purchases do not require a permit:

• Purchase of separate apartments.

- Purchase of real estate by a foreigner living in Poland for at least five years who has a permanent residence visa.

- Purchase of real estate by a foreigner married to a Polish citizen and living in Poland for two years.

- Purchase of real estate by legal entities for statutory purposes of lots not larger than 0.4 hectares (1 acre) in urban areas.

However, exemption from the obligation to obtain a permit does not apply to real estate located in border zones and agricultural land of an area of over one hectare. Regarding any other form of real estate transaction, "a foreign investor must be licensed to do business in Poland (a condition which is automatically met by all registered companies), and justify his actual need for the acquisition of the property."

Matters connected with permissions are handled by:

- **Ministerstwo Spraw Wewnetrznych i Administracji** (the Ministry of Internal Affairs and Administration), *ul. Stefana Batorego 5, 02-591 Warszawa; tel. (48)22- 621-2020; fax (48)22-849-74-94; website: (in Polish) www.mswia.gov.pl.*

Polish realtor contacts

- **Ober-Haus** (Darek Karbowniczak), *ul. Krolewska 14, 00-950 Warszawa; tel. (48)22- 8291212; fax (48)22-8291222; e-mail: darek.karbowniczak@ober-haus.com; website: www.ober-haus.pl.* The address in Warsaw is the flagship office, but Ober-Haus is a large group with a presence in a number of Polish cities as well as in the Baltics. The Kraków agency is at *Stawkowska 6, 31-014 Kraków; tel. (48)12-428-17-00; fax (48)12-428-19-00; e-mail: krakow@ober-haus.com.*

- **Popieluch Nieruchomosci** (Piotr Popieluch), *ul. Krupowki 27, 34-500 Zakopane; tel. (48)18-2000-160; fax (48)18-201-2702; e-mail: popieluch@nieruchomosci.zakopane.pl; website: www. nieruchomosci.zakopane.pl.*

Buying property in Poland

Additional costs associated with buying property are a 5% transfer tax and around 3% for agency fees.

Annual property tax rates are established by local councils and are subject to an annual maximum set by the government. That maximum for residential buildings is PZL 0.51 (13 cents) per square meter of floor space. If you own a 1,075-square-foot apartment, your tax will be around $13! For buildings connected with business activities and for the part of residential buildings occupied for business purposes, the maximum is PZL 17.31 ($4.50) per square meter of floor space.

There are plans for a new cadastral tax to replace the current real estate tax, but it will not take effect until 2006 at the earliest. Indications are that it will run at 0.1% of a property's value.

Paying your taxes

If you have income from Polish sources (or if your stay exceeds 183 days in a given tax year), you will be liable for Polish income tax. However, as Poland has double taxation agreements with a number of countries (including the U.S.) you should not be subject to two doses of tax.

Income tax rates are progressive—there are three rates: 19%, 30%, and 40%. Each individual has an allowance of 530.08 zlotys ($140). The tax is assessed as follows:

- Up to PZL 37,024 ($9,665)—19%

- PZL 37,024 ($9,665) to PZL 74,048 ($19,325)—30%

- Over PZL 74,048 ($19,325)—40%

Capital gains from the sale of real estate are taxed at a 10% flat rate if the sale occurs within a five-year period from the end of the year in which the acquisition is made. After five years, any gain is tax-exempt.

At present there is a capital gains tax exemption on profits made in the Polish stock market. The Polish finance minister was recently reported as saying a tax would probably be introduced in 2004, but as we go to press, a final decision had not yet been made.

Notes:

Notes:

Notes: